SONYA RICHMOND

How to be Healthy
with Yoga

BELL PUBLISHING COMPANY, INC.

New York

BELL PUBLISHING COMPANY, INC.

FOR MY PARENTS, BELL AND DAVID

with my love

This edition published by
Bell Publishing Company, Inc.,
a division of Crown Publishers, Inc.,
by arrangement with Arco Books, Inc.
A   B   C   D   E   F   G

PRINTED IN THE UNITED STATES OF AMERICA

Contents

List of Illustrations

CHAPTER ONE

What Yoga can do

YOGA at last is coming into its own in the Western world. After many years of being dismissed as a bizarre cult attractive only to eccentrics, it is today recognized as a fundamental art and skill. More than that, many of its most bitter opponents, people who were among the first to cry down Yogic culture, have now embraced it as a way of life.

The ancients who formulated the science of Yoga were way ahead of us in our modern world of stress and hurry. Recognizing, thousands of years ago, man's basic need for discipline to counteract the physical and spiritual deterioration caused by the mere fight for survival, they evolved a science which is at once as ancient as India herself and as modern as the space age.

The law of Yoga is the law of Life. Yoga embodies the secrets of successful living and combines profound and age-old truths with a way of life acceptable to the modern mind. It was evolved from the Veda, one of the most ancient scriptural books known to mankind in which Indian saints and sages taught that the Universe is one and that all religions are paths ascending the same mountain towards Eternal Truth. The great modern saint, Sri Ramakrishna, is often quoted as saying, 'As many faiths, so many paths.'

But Yoga is not a religion, nor is it a mystic cult. It is a Hindu system of philosophic meditation and asceticism designed to effect the reunion of the devotee's soul with God. It is a philosophy which integrates the individual life and the world surrounding us to achieve a basic harmony and equilibrium in the heart and mind of man.

How is physical health a part of so spiritual a philosophy as Yoga? Simply that the trichotomy of our lives, divided into body, soul and spirit, is echoed in the complete Yogic philosophy whose three approaches—asana (posture), pranayama (breath control), and meditation—are unified as one approach to self discovery.

One of the fundamental doctrines of Yoga is that God is *within* each one of us but He reveals Himself only in conditions of purity, both spiritually and physically. To function on a higher level, either mentally or physically, the first step must always be to rid the body of the impurities that cause disease and which impede spiritual development. One can draw the analogy of the window which must be cleaned before one can see the light clearly through it.

This basic principle of purification underlines all Yogic practice and at the same time it aims at establishing a balance in the body so that it functions, as it were, like a perfect machine. When this state of physical balance is achieved the mind can then be controlled and can realize the ultimate in pure thought and reason. I have yet to meet anyone who can successfully employ the techniques of mind control while plagued with indigestion, asthma, a thumping headache or any other of the ills and stress symptoms which plague modern man. So first things first. Physical ills drag one downwards and the disciplinary science of Hatha Yoga was evolved that the body would be freed from pain and disease.

This book is primarily concerned with this Yoga of the physical body known as Hatha Yoga. While the body and the mind cannot be separated and the health of one affects the health of the other, I have laid stress on the day to day problems and ailments of the average person who wishes to improve his general health. Not everyone has the mystic vocation to achieve union with God, the Universal Spirit, which is the primary aim of all Yoga, but everyone would like to know how to improve his health.

Many Westerners, moving as they do in a world of hurry and stress, feel that Yoga holds nothing for them and that the whole philosophy is rather remote, vague, and impractical. In this book my aim is to show readers how the ancient system of Yoga provides an effective answer to the many problems of our modern life. You can take an active part in the hurly burly of everyday living and Yoga will act as a protection from the numerous stresses of your environment. While best results are obtained by exercising and practising breathing and relaxation alone, nevertheless you need not become a hermit to achieve success and improved health through Hatha Yoga.

Recognizing then that you are not a mystic and you do not wish to spend years in meditation and mental discipline to find the true meaning of God and Life, how then can Yoga help *you*? Let us consider your problems. Are you overworked and tense and do you find it impossible to relax even in bed at night? Are you overweight yet lack the will-power to diet? Do you sometimes find yourself unable to cope with the dash and tumult of everyday life? Are you irritable, worried, nervous? Are you plagued by indigestion and other stress symptoms? Or simply do you seek something, you know not what, which goes above and beyond the superficial level of everyday living?

Yoga awaits your interest, your inspection, your first hesitant experiments. It is here, it has always been here, it is yours for the taking. Those who have delved into its profound philosophy and studied for years with patience and devotion to learn more and more have found something unique, priceless, and indestructible.

The uninformed often speak of Yoga as some dark, hidden practice of magical rites for attaining wondrous powers. While it is an indisputable fact that some advanced Yogis are indeed possessed of such powers, they reached their state of heightened consciousness, not by bell, book, and candle, but by the disciplining of the mind for which the first step is the perfecting of the physical body, through Hatha Yoga.

The inner power of Yoga becomes apparent when one realizes that it has something to offer every thinking person, here and now, yet it is an ancient Hindu philosophy, its beginnings shrouded in the mists of time. The idea may sound fanciful but the proof is manifold.

Hatha Yoga is the preparation for all the higher forms of Yoga and, because of its benefits to the body and the mind, it is the most popular form of Yoga and the most acceptable to Western habits of thought. At the same time it is the most misunderstood science on the face of the earth. Many well-meaning, but misguided individuals have a disparaging attitude towards Hatha Yoga, because its special province is the physical body. But the sages who formulated the disciplinary science of Hatha Yoga recognized that the first thing man desires and needs is health, so they devised the best means of attaining and preserving it. While Hatha Yoga is the cause of much apprehension among people who effect to despise things physical and concentrate on higher matters, it has always been a source of interest to me how anyone can meditate on Higher Things while doubled up with pain or suffering any kind of physical discomfort.

Having declared then that Hatha Yoga can help you towards better health and calm your mind so that you can solve your personal problems, I do want to stress two facts. Firstly, that the aim of Hatha Yoga is *not* the acquisition of a superior muscular physique but the *discipline* and the *purification* of the body that we may forget our earthly shell enough to reach a state of heightened awareness through the control of the mind. Secondly, that Hatha Yoga is neither the easiest nor the fastest system of physical culture to show results. Why then Hatha Yoga for your health? Why not weight lifting, club swinging, athletics, or even dancing? All of these will improve the circulation, the figure, and strengthen the muscles. What has Hatha Yoga to offer in addition to this? Simply that Hatha will provide an extraordinary control over the body and awaken the mind and spirit, the higher self if you like, as no purely physical culture system could possibly do. Also, the above-mentioned activities are beyond the capabilities of a large section of the community, the aged, the infirm, the lame, and the physically frail. Those activities involve violent movement whereas Hatha Yoga is essentially a static science. Basically one gets into a Yoga posture or asana and remains so for as long as possible. Stress is laid on pressure of certain organs, glands and muscles rather than on movement. When movement is necessary in Hatha Yoga it is always gentle and graceful, therefore anyone can benefit from Yoga regardless of age, sex, race, walk of life, or religious belief. It is a *universal* science. It can lead to more abundant living and a new awareness of higher things through ridding your body of the pains and diseases which drag your mind back into the earth when it wants to wing its way upwards towards the light.

It is reported that Lord Buddha, whose philosophy is based on the Veda from which Yoga was evolved, said that the first step on the way to spiritual freedom and salvation is perfect physical health. So if you are drawn towards Hatha Yoga do not be put off by others who might tell you that you will never reach a state of heightened consciousness by turning your body upside down or sitting in various leg-breaking postures. Tell them that if the blood is impure then the brain, the nerves, the psycho-spiritual life, yes even the *thoughts*, cannot but be affected. Tell them that a man cannot control his mind until his body is made pure and healthy. Even if you do not aim at mental discipline, and many of you I know do not, you can with persistent practice improve your general health beyond belief.

You will find that Yoga knowledge, once accumulated, will begin to influence and help you in your daily life, whoever you may be. It will gradually invade every part of your life, from your attitude towards your fellow men to the way you sleep, breathe, think, and even eat. Did I say eat? What has eating to do with Hatha Yoga? It has very much to do with it. It is a strange fact that Yoga's doctrine of non-violence very soon influences even the most enthusiastic meat-eater to think again about a vegetarian diet. As the senses become more acute through the practice of Yoga, one begins to experience a distaste for all forms of killing and violence. Meat becomes unpalatable because many devotees of Yoga are actually able to see the astral bodies of the slaughtered animals as they tuck into a thick, juicy steak. Their senses gradually becoming awakened, they think on things that never occurred to them before and in the case of slaughtering helpless animals they begin to understand and revolt at the hideous practices that go on in abattoirs all over the world. So you have been warned! You, who are reading a book on Yoga for perhaps the first time in your life, you who have eaten and enjoyed meat and fish for many years and intend to go on doing so, you will suddenly discover, if you practise Yoga, that meat is not quite so delicious as you hitherto thought and that other foods, cheese and vegetables and fruits, taste much better.

You see it is impossible to practise Hatha Yoga as a kind of hobby and hope to keep it aside from your everyday life, like knitting or woodwork. Inevitably it must influence your whole life and thought and make you, not a different person or even a better one, but into your *real self* denuded of all false pretence, of false values, and of unreasonable fears and inhibitions. If I have alarmed you in any way or made you feel that Yoga is going to prove far too complicated a thing in your orderly life, let me hasten to assure you that the influence of Yoga cannot be otherwise than beneficial. While Yoga is not, as I stressed at the beginning, a religion, nevertheless those men who devote their whole lives to it become saintly and intensely spiritual. This applies to devotees of Hatha as well as the other Yogas which proves conclusively that though Hatha's province is the physical body and its perfection, in the last analysis Hatha Yoga is a *spiritual* discipline.

You may consider Hatha Yoga either as a special subject in itself or as an adjunct to other forms of Yoga. Whatever your reason (and there can never be a bad reason for doing something good) Yoga can help you with your everyday problems on all levels. As you grow healthier and more relaxed you become more gentle, less inclined to fits of irritation and temper. Yoga provides the counter-weight so urgently needed to the ever increasing nervous, mental and physical tensions of our modern life.

All the exercises or asanas of Hatha Yoga are based on the formula of stretching, relaxing, deep breathing and increasing the circulation of the blood and the powers of concentration. Yogic culture is divided into eight sections.

1. Yama—ethics.
2. Niyama—religious observances.
3. Asana—postures.
4. Pranayama—breathing exercises and control of the breath.
5. Pratyahara—withdrawing of the senses from external objects.

6. Dhyarana—concentration.
7. Dhyana—meditation.
8. Samadhi—super-consciousness.

It is with 3 and 4 that this book is primarily concerned for these sections are the beginning of all Yoga without which you cannot hope to gain mastery over yourself and learn the secrets of the Universe. According to the Yoga Shastras the Yoga asanas total the staggering number of 840,000, but the important ones number only 84. Of these I have described all but the most difficult. This is a book primarily for the Westerner and the beginner in Yoga and as such it does not contain postures suitable only to advanced students who are able to practise many hours a day. The asanas included in this book will suffice to bring the health of the average person to a far higher level than hitherto experienced and, combined with the other practices described in this book, will open out a new horizon beyond the banalities of everyday existence.

Let me warn you that Yoga is another word for hard work, indeed some say it is all work and no play. That may be so, but all the same if you have read thus far your mind must be searching for something and if that something is Yoga then you will not be deterred by the mere thought of hard work. Rather you will glory in it for there is a sense of great achievement in self-discipline. Yes, Hatha Yoga is discipline all the way. I can show you the path up the mountain but it is up to you to climb. With the best will in the world I cannot do the hard work for you. But if you choose this path all you need to follow it is determination. If you have it you cannot fail. If you lack it you cannot begin.

'There is an innermost centre in us all
Where Truth abides in fullness; and to know
Rather consists in opening out a way
Whence the imprisoned splendour may escape . . .'
(BROWNING)

CHAPTER TWO

Relaxation and stretching

No one, I think, would disagree with me when I say that the pace of modern life, especially in the big cities, is destructive. Why, but *why* is everyone intent on doing something all the time? Do they imagine they are missing something if they go to bed with a book, or sit and think, or just sit? Some people cannot tolerate being alone. Their own company is inexpressibly boring and depressing. But why? If only these unfortunates could catch even a solitary glimpse of the rich inner life of the spirit, and the awesome power of *clear* thought.

People who rush about in a frenzy are often not the ones who get the best results. What about the man who has had the time to think? Who has *made* the time to think? While others rushed dizzily past him he has been evolving ideas, building and planning in his slow but constructive mind. It has been said that much of the good work of the world has been done by the dull man who has done his best.

Yoga will not teach you to be dull, rather the contrary it will teach you to be more magnetic, but it *will* show you the importance of knowing when to slow down. The ancient Chinese believed in the theory of 'masterly inactivity' and this served to lay down the foundation of a unique civilization. By 'inactivity' I do not mean idleness, laziness or mental inertia. Yoga is not for the lazy. No, Yoga's inactivity serves as a breathing space among the bustle of everyday life so that one can recharge the batteries of one's physical and mental processes to pursue life with renewed energy and clearer thought.

Yogis realized, centuries ago, that the mind always functions better in a state of relaxation. Force yourself to work and the result is a headache, weariness, and a lack of spontaneity. In those fields of work where creative ability is constantly called into play this spontaneity is of vital importance. No one wants

14

to read, hear, or look at something dragged from a fogged and tired brain.

Yoga's first lesson, then, is how to relax. I do not wish to be an alarmist but the sheer inability to relax sends many millions of people to their graves ten, twenty, sometimes forty years before their time. So let us first consider how you are, here and now, going to cheat the undertaker of those precious years of your valuable time.

First of all do not confuse relaxation with inertia. Relaxation has been defined as 'a conscious transfer of energy from one department of nature to another after an extreme tension of body and brain'. A mere change of occupation is a form of relaxation. This is why many office workers play football or tennis at weekends, why many manual workers sit and watch television, why many 'brain' workers have hobbies that involve working with the hands.

For your first lesson in relaxation let us consider that mid-morning cup of tea that most people look forward to. What do you do when it arrives? Stand and gulp it down and maybe throw another one down your throat after it? Try again. No matter who you are, a busy housewife and mother, a secretary, a company director, a cabinet minister, or a ballet dancer, *stop* when that cup of tea arrives. Stop whatever you are doing, sit down quietly even if all hell is let loose around you, and enjoy that cup of tea. Drink it slowly. Try to forget, even if you have only five minutes to do so, all your immediate cares—the shopping, the laundry, that lost letter, that copy your editor is screaming for, that order you forgot to push out. Let it wait. What is the very worst thing that can happen if you drink a cup of tea in peace and quiet? Why nothing. And how much better you will feel for it, how much easier things will seem after your few moments' respite. Relax periodically and you double your efficiency. If you doubt me then try it and see.

But this is a book about Hatha Yoga so you will want to know the Yoga way to relax. Lie down on the floor and let go. That is all. And that is Yoga? It is indeed. It is called SAVASANA or the CORPSE POSTURE. Not a very pleasant name I agree but all the same it is one of Yoga's most valuable and powerful weapons against ill health and stress. It is pictured in figure 1.

Try it. Lie down on the floor, no pillows, just a rug or the carpet. Leave off your shoes and wear as little clothing as possible. Whatever you wear must be light and loose fitting. Now stretch your arms above your head and stretch out your legs and feet. Go on, have a good stretch like your cat does before it settles down to sleep. Close your eyes and let your head roll to one side. Let your hands flop where they will and imagine that your body has no bones and that you are giving your whole weight to the floor. Imagine you are on a cloud and that your body is slowly sinking through it. Keep your eyes closed and think of something peaceful, a lovely piece of music perhaps or the sound of the sea. Put on a soothing record if you like or open the window and listen to the birds. Tell yourself that you are drowsy and comfortable over and over again.

Now then, what about those knots of tense muscles around your mouth, your eyes, your stomach and your legs? Go over all areas of your body and locate any knots of tension there might be. Be stern with them. Make them loosen up. Very likely they will tighten up again as soon as your back is turned so to speak but keep your mind's eye open and consciously and repeatedly relax any clenched muscles. The worst offenders by far are the muscles of the face. You are clenching your teeth and your jaws right now are you not? You would be surprised at the number of people who do that, even in their sleep. The counter measure is yawning. Do it as often as you can but do please choose appropriate times as yawning is not socially acceptable in many circles and your commendable efforts to teach your facial muscles to relax might be misinterpreted! Open your mouth as wide as you can, stretch your jaws, tense your facial muscles and then suddenly relax them. Keep practising that movement and you will soon rid yourself of teeth clenching. That in itself is a good start.

So you are lying on the floor in the Corpse Posture and you are finding that it isn't as easy as it looks to relax. It is easy to lie down on the floor but you think I am unreasonable to ask

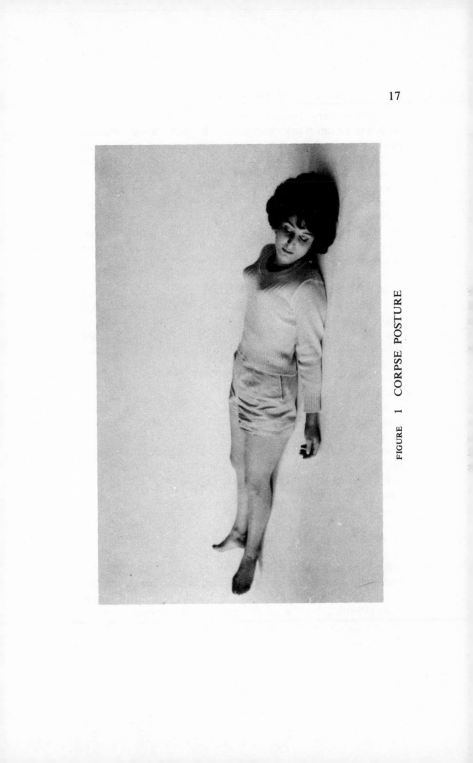

FIGURE 1 CORPSE POSTURE

you to relax every muscle, do you not? But it can be done. I can do it and so can many other people. It takes constant practice but how worthwhile is time spent towards this end for Savasana is one of the greatest vitalizers known to man. Perform it whenever you are tired, angry, upset, or brain-fagged. Perform it whenever things get on top of you. It is not time wasted. It is Yoga's 'masterly inactivity' working for you.

No one is too madly busy to be quite unable to practise the art of relaxation at least once a day. Give to it a little of your time and it will repay you a thousandfold. What about those few minutes before you get into bed at night? Are you too busy then?

When you have made some progress with Savasana your feet will be set firmly on the Yoga path. Its great influence will begin to work for you. As you grow more and more able to smooth away the tensions in your body you will find that the tensions in your mind will also become less. Problems which seemed mountainous will, if you practise and perfect the art of relaxation, be reduced to a size whereby you can cope with and overcome them.

But to return to you lying on the floor and thinking yourself into relaxing those tense muscles. What about that *mind* of yours running round in circles? What about that eye of yours on the clock? What about that nagging worry at the back of your mind that you should be up and about *doing* things? No, you are not really relaxing at all. Let us try again. Let us approach Savasana from another angle.

I want you to learn to stretch. A simple enough request but, you may ask, is this Yoga too? Just—stretching? It is indeed. As you read this book it will become more and more apparent to you that although Yoga is a Hindu science three thousand years old, a spiritually based way of life, a contemplative philosophy and a profoundly dedicated art, nevertheless it has a real and vital place in modern everyday life, your life. A simple thing like stretching is as much a part of Yoga as any of the more complicated postures which I will describe during the course of this book.

Stretching then. Lie down as before on your back with your legs and feet together and raise your arms above your head with the fingers interlaced. Now turn your hands palms upwards and you will immediately feel the increased stretch along your ribs and back. Stretch your arms as far above your head as you can and at the same time point your toes and push them forward so that you feel the tension in every part of your legs, arms and shoulders.

Concentrate on stretching thus far and when, after practising a few times, you can fully tense your arms, shoulders and legs simultaneously, try at the same time to pull in your stomach muscles, arch your spine, and to complete the picture open your mouth in a gigantic yawn. You will not make a particularly aesthetic picture at this moment but remember that Yoga should always be practised alone and in silence, if possible in secrecy. It is not a science for the extrovert. So you can go ahead and pull faces to your heart's content and if no one is any the wiser you and your health will be all the better for it.

Having stretched every part of your body, suddenly let go. Remember that you must stretch everything you can to the *utmost*, before you let go, so that the ensuing relaxation will be all the more complete. And when you let go you are once more in Savasana but this time you should feel much more relaxed. But keep a wary eye open for those persistent offenders—eyes, lips, teeth, and tongue. Are you clenching them again? Train your mind to watch these key points throughout the day not only when you are practising Savasana, and if you discover that you are clenching any of your facial muscles be stern with them. As I have reiterated, they need constant watching but your persistence will soon be rewarded not only in a new feeling of relaxation but also in your appearance. For Yoga is a beauty treatment too. Those little tension lines around your eyes, lips, and between the eyebrows will not be given a chance to develop into deep, ineradicable wrinkles. Yoga, and particularly Savasana is the simple secret of how devotees of Yoga remain miraculously young looking even when well advanced in years, for nothing is so ageing as stress. It puts lines on to the face, sends the eyes back into their sockets, and gives an ageing droop to the figure.

Having approached Savasana from two different angles, let us try a third. Yoga, while based on a set of unchanging principles, is not dogmatic and there is much room for personal preference and capabilities. Yoga's greatness lies in its ability to recognize every individual and not lump humanity together as so many other sciences do. Savasana, then, from a third angle. This one is rather more difficult but you may find it rather fun. It is called the *Angle Balance* and you will see an illustration of it in figure 33. It is not as easy as it looks but it is well worth your perseverance.

Angle Balance

Lie flat on your back with your hands at your sides, and legs together. Now raise your head and shoulders off the floor and at the same time raise your legs with your knees bent until you can grasp your toes. Now very carefully straighten your knees still holding your toes until you are in the position illustrated in figure 33. Hold this position for as long as you can and then suddenly flop back on to the floor. Again you are in Savasana and the ensuing relaxation will be more complete after the preceding tension and concentration required by the ANGLE BALANCE.

This first Yoga asana, the Corpse Posture, is one of the most important and although you may be itching to learn something a little more spectacular I do want to impress on you that stretching and relaxation is the beginning of all Yoga. It calms the mind and renews the body with energy and the life force which is known as PRANA. So do practise Savasana wherever and whenever you possibly can.

Many people make their first mistake of the day the moment they open their eyes in the morning, and they start a chain reaction which echoes throughout the day. They open their eyes, look at the clock, and *leap* out of bed in a frenzy. The poor human body is built to withstand an appalling amount of abuse but to subject it to this kind of punishment, day after day, is simply courting trouble. Think what happens to your nervous system when you wake up and hurl yourself out of bed in the morning. Shock and an unspeakable buffeting. Is it necessary? Give yourself a little time to return to this world from the threshold of another. Set your alarm clock just five minutes earlier than usual, try this Yoga waking up routine, and see the difference to your whole day.

Waking up Routine

The word stretching is reiterated throughout this book and it crops up here too, first thing in the morning. Stretch up your arms with your fingers interlaced and palms upwards, stretch your legs, open your mouth wide and yawn several times. As you lie in bed, still half asleep, keep on yawning and stretching like a cat and then finally relax your body and do the following leg stretching exercise.

Leg stretching exercise

This is very simple. While lying in bed with your feet together push one of your legs down towards the bottom of the bed as though you were trying to lengthen it. Point your toes and you will feel a pull from your hip right down to your heel. Hold this position for one minute only and then relax. If you haven't a clock with a minute hand then simply count to sixty as you push your leg forward. After a moment's rest repeat the exercise with the other leg. As this is a very potent exercise for the nerves do not repeat it more than once at a time for each leg. It may be repeated when you go to bed at night if you so wish.

After the Leg Stretching exercise very *slowly* get out of bed, stretch once more with your arms above your head and I assure you that your usual morning half dead feeling will be conspicuous by its absence.

I will end your first lesson in stretching and relaxation by describing an exercise taken from the ancient system of SOORYA NAMASKAR OR SUN EXERCISE because it is practised facing the sun as it rises, or at least in the early morning. There are twelve positions which bring flexibility to the spine which is so vital if one is to perform the more strenuous Yoga asanas. Of the twelve, which stretch various ligaments and give different movements to the vertebral column, I have selected a series of five which the average reader will not find beyond his capabilities. In this series a full round constitutes nine movements, that is five forward movements and four retracing ones.

Soorya Namaskar or Sun Exercise

1. Stand erect, feet together, hands at your sides. Take a deep slow breath, raise your arms above your head with the fingers interlaced and then bend backwards as far as you can without overbalancing. (See Fig. 8, page 39.)

2. Now exhale as completely as you can and at the same time bend forward and place your palms flat on the floor about four or five inches in front of your toes. Keep your knees absolutely straight. The correct position is shown in figure 2.

One important feature of the SUN EXERCISE is the chin lock, which simply means pressing your chin tightly against your chest. The Yogis maintain that this has a beneficial effect on the thyroid glands. Remember while performing the SUN EXERCISE to maintain the chin lock through stages 2, 3, 4, 6, 7, and 8.

3. Inhale again, step back with the right foot as in figure 3 so that the other knee is bent and the chin lock is maintained.

4. Exhale once more and move the other leg back as in figure 4, keeping the knees as rigid as possible and trying to reach the floor with your heels. This is not possible of course but the action of trying to reach the floor with the heels will increase the pull on the calves and thighs. Remember to maintain the chin lock.

5. Inhale again, slowly and deeply and at the same time release the chin lock and, while keeping the upper part of the body as steady as possible, lower the legs and abdomen *slowly*. Balance throughout stage 5 on the toes and palms until you are in the cobra-like position in figure 5. Arch your back as fully as possible, keep your knees rigid and press back your neck and your head while keeping your arms straight. Only your palms and your toes should touch the floor.

6. Having performed the five exercises you must now retrace your steps to the starting position thus: from stage 5 assume the position in figure 4 with the body making a bridge. (Page 23.)

2 3

FIGURES 2, 3, 4, 5   SUN EXERCISE

4 5

23

7. Bring one leg forward as in figure 3.

8. Bring forward the other leg and you are now bending forward with your palms flat on the floor as in figure 2.

9. Very slowly straighten up, take a deep breath and then lie down for a few moments and relax.

It may take you a little time to perfect the Sun Exercise, as it has taken you some little time to read it and look at the illustrations but the actual performance of it should take you no more than sixty seconds if done correctly. It is not really complicated and once you have learned the simple sequence of movements they should follow one another with fluid simplicity. Nothing should be hurried. Every movement of the sun exercise should be held for as long as possible before proceeding to the next.

The benefits are manifold. Soorya Namaskar stretches the spine in several directions and helps to keep it supple. It stretches and contracts the abdomen and so helps to relieve congestion and constipation. It tones and limbers up the muscles and has a bracing effect on the entire body. Soorya Namaskar is one of the most complete and beneficial exercises in the whole Yoga range and should never be omitted from your practice schedule.

I will now outline a schedule for those of you who are convinced that you cannot find the time to practise Yoga asanas. It requires but twelve minutes but if you can find more time in which to practise so much the better.

1. Leg stretching exercise, sixty seconds each leg   2 minutes
2. Savasana or Corpse Posture preceded by concentration on relaxing muscles, tension of muscles or Angle Balance   5 minutes
3. Sun Exercise performed slowly four times   4 minutes

The extra minute is to give you time to wake up. Twelve minutes is so very little time out of your whole day but you may soon find that these minutes become the most important part of your day because of your increased feeling of relaxation and well being. In time that alarm going off twelve minutes early will not seem like a monster but more like a welcome friend.

CHAPTER THREE

Tension and emotional stress

You are not alone, you who are tense, nervous, worried, unable to relax even in bed. You seem to be tied up in knots and you sometimes feel at your screaming wits' end. And you take relaxation pills, pep pills, tranquillizers, anything to give you a 'lift' and then wonder at the resulting unpleasant side effects. Can Yoga help? But of course it can. Yoga doesn't like drugs and you know, your body does not either so if the so-called orthodox methods have failed to establish an easing of tension in your overworked body and over-worried mind then why not try Yoga's way? Yoga has often been known to succeed when medicine has failed.

Proper breathing is intrinsically linked with relaxation, with the emotions, with the health of the body itself. The thoughts are reflections of the breathing habits and so if the breathing is faulty then the mind cannot but be affected. You can prove this for yourself by your day to day experiences. When you are absorbed in a book, watching television, or listening to an interesting talk on the radio your breathing processes become slow. When your mind is afflicted by anger, or sorrow, the breath becomes irregular and choppy. When you are frightened you gasp and hold your breath, and when you are bored you open your mouth and yawn.

The exercises formulated by the Yogis of ancient times in connection with the respiratory tract are all based on a close observation of the body's natural impulses. This most vital of the body's functions is so neglected by the average person that the majority of people take in only enough oxygen to keep themselves from falling dead.

Mind and breath, then, being interdependent, you must learn how to breathe properly if you want to calm your mind and rid yourself of your worries and frustrations in everyday life. When

25

you are at peace your breath is slow and even so if you reverse the process and learn to breathe slowly and deeply your mind will follow suit. You cannot be worried and upset if you are breathing in a calm and controlled manner, nor can you be calm if your breath is coming in hurried jerks.

So first things first. I want you to try the Yoga COMPLETE BREATH which employs the lower, middle and upper lung. It is sometimes divided into three—diaphragmatic, intercostal, and clavicular breathing—but in its correct form the Yoga COMPLETE BREATH should employ all three sections in one fluid intake of breath. Beginners should take things very easily at first. Lie down flat on the floor, no pillows, and place your hands lightly over your diaphragm. Remember to wear nothing tight around your waist or chest, and women should always loosen the bra before doing any Yoga breathing exercise.

The Complete Breath

1. Slowly exhale as completely as you can.

2. Very slowly inhale through the mouth, drawing in the air evenly and without sudden jerks. With your hands placed lightly over your diaphragm you will find that this is the first area to expand.

3. As your inhalation progresses you will feel a very slight retraction of your lower abdomen.

4. As you complete your inhalation you will feel your shoulders rise slightly as your upper lung becomes fully expanded.

5. Slowly exhale through the mouth, using slight force. Contract the abdomen as you complete your exhalation to expel as much air as possible.

Lie quietly for a few minutes after you have taken your first Complete Breath. Do not attempt to sit up for a while or you may experience a slight dizziness or faintness due to hyperventilation caused by a sudden, excessive, and unaccustomed intake of oxygen. If you do have such a reaction it only proves how badly your poor lungs needed that extra oxygen, but do not worry, the dizzy feeling will soon pass. Go carefully at first with this exercise and soon you will be able to perform it with no unpleasant side effects. When you reach this stage you can perform the exercise sitting up straight with your head level and your hands in your lap, or even standing erect with your hands at your sides. Always, of course, practise Yoga breathing exercises before an open window and if at all possible, in the open air. For the first few days do not take more than two Yoga Complete Breaths a day, but gradually increase the number *ad lib* up to sixty full breaths a day. This should be a slow process and you should allow yourself quite some time before attempting the full quota of sixty a day. Be content at first to take just a few at a time.

When performing the Complete Breath I want you to be conscious of the slow filling up of your lungs, from the abdomen to the shoulders, and the ensuing slow exhalation should produce a feeling of calmness and relaxation in your body and in your mind. Never hurry this exercise. It is far better to take two slow correct Complete Breaths than to take ten hurried ones. In Yoga exercises it is always quality and not quantity that counts.

Tense people will particularly benefit from this exercise if they perform it just before bedtime as it promotes healthy, natural and refreshing sleep. When you are able to perform it correctly do try to practise it whenever you can during the day but particularly when you feel tired, depressed or upset. You even take a few deep breaths as you take that morning walk up to the bus stop or the train, in which case you can match your breathing to your footsteps, say breathe in for six and exhale for six. If you are lucky enough to be anywhere near the sea draw in that wonderful, sweet-smelling air for all you are worth.

It is said that some people are tense by nature. Not true. They are tense by sheer bad habit, and these so-called natural-tension-merchants unconsciously allow all kinds of lurking tensions to accumulate until, hey presto! a beautiful, full-blown peptic ulcer, a chronic heart condition or worse. The breaking up of tension is going to be, for most people, the breaking of the habit of a lifetime. I have been told in all seriousness many times, 'But, Miss Richmond, I must build up tension while I am working otherwise . . .' Otherwise what? Otherwise, I would add, you would have so much more energy that you wouldn't know what to do with it, so you feel you must squander a little by becoming tense!

Let us consider this problem in its proper perspective. No one, repeat, no one ever got the best out of themselves by means of tension. You may think you need it, that you could not do without it, nevertheless you wonder sometimes why you are unable to sleep and that your nerves are often 'worn to shreds', and you suffer from nameless fears. Can you imagine what it would be like to be free for ever of these distressing symptoms, to feel relaxed and cheerful and full of energy? I can show you the way, through Yoga, but there is a price. You will have to part with those precious tensions of yours.

My intention in this book is to show you the way to better health through Yoga and not to moralize in any way, but may I tell you just one story which I hope might stick in your mind for the rest of your life? It is aimed particularly at those readers who feel they cannot live without a burden of tension on their shoulders.

There was once a wise old man who was sitting at the window of his house when he saw, down in the street below, a poor beggar carrying a heavy load on his back. 'What is that you carry?' called the old man. The beggar looked up at the window and then opened up the large sack he was carrying. It contained bundles of old newspapers, empty bottles, bits of wood, empty tins, broken bricks and all kinds of useless matter. 'But it is nothing but a lot of rubbish,' protested the old man, 'tell me, why do you burden yourself with it?' To which the beggar replied, 'I must, it is all I have'.

And now to the second round in this battle against those tensions of yours. In the previous chapter I discussed physical relaxation, yawning and stretching, and if you have been practising the exercises I described they will have gone a long way towards the breaking up of tension. Let us now go a step farther. Your next task is to learn how to develop and control your respiration. In Yoga breathing the following five principles are involved:

1. The habitual use of the full power of the lungs.
2. Retention of the breath.
3. Cleansing of the lungs and bronchial passages.
4. Breathing and slow stretching.
5. Alternate breathing, or breathing through one nostril at a time. This is known as 'Sun and Moon' breathing.

In this book I will cover all five principles of Yoga breathing and in this chapter I will deal with 1, 2, and 5. Firstly, then, practise the Yoga Complete Breath as often as you can and always remember that the depth and quality of your breathing is far more important than the number of breaths you take. It is a good idea to start your Pranayama or breathing exercises by taking a few full breaths to cleanse your lungs and prepare yourself for the other breathing exercises, all of which are basically variations of the Complete Breath. Practise the Complete Breath in any position you prefer, either lying down, sitting on the floor with your spine straight, sitting on a hard chair with your hands in your lap, or standing up straight.

Retention of the Breath
This should not be attempted until you are able to perform the Complete Breath at least half a dozen times in succession without experiencing any unpleasant dizziness or fainting. Then proceed as follows. When you have completed your inhalation hold your breath for an instant before you start to exhale. One second is enough at first, but gradually extend this period of retention until you can hold your breath for several seconds without discomfort and without employing any force. Please do not try to force your lungs to do things which you know they would rather not. Remember that correct Yoga breathing is based on the body's *natural* impulses.

At the end of every exhalation there is a natural pause with the lungs completely empty. At first you must obey this natural impulse and breathe in when you feel the need to, but gradually extend this pause for a second longer, and then yet another second, but do not force the pace. This gradual extension of the pause will make the ensuing inhalation that much more full and deep. Practise retention of the breath until you can perform it to your satisfaction but I repeat s-l-o-w is the word for Yoga breathing, slow and rhythmic. The word hurry has no place whatever in this book.

Alternate Breathing

I would like you now to try Alternate Breathing or, as it is also called, SUN AND MOON BREATHING.

To explain this strange name before you begin, the two aspects of Prana or life force which surrounds us are personified as Pingala, the positive pole and Ida, the negative pole. One of the aims of Yoga is to balance their opposite currents in the body, which then produces a state of perfect spiritual and mental equilibrium. The breath that enters the right nostril or Pingala is called the sun breath and that which enters the Ida or left nostril is the moon breath. The ALTERNATE BREATH consists of deep controlled breathing through each nostril in turn.

Sit down either cross-legged on the floor or on a hard chair with your spine erect, but not stiff, and your head level. Close your eyes and proceed as follows:

1. Close your left nostril with your left thumb and breathe in, slowly and deeply, through the right nostril.

2. Hold the breath for two seconds.

3. Close the right nostril with the last two fingers of your left hand and exhale very slowly through the left nostril.

4. A natural pause will follow and when the impulse to inhale appears do so, this time through the left nostril, the right still being held closed.

5. Hold the breath for two seconds.

6. Exhale slowly through the right nostril with the left held closed.

This completes one round. Beginners to Pranayama should limit themselves to two rounds at first, but do add one round each week until you are performing six rounds a day. Ideally this exercise should be performed facing different points of the compass according to the time of day, following the path of the sun. Thus in the early morning you should perform it facing east, at midday facing the meridian, at sunset facing the west, and at night facing the north. SUN AND MOON BREATHING should be preceded and followed by three or four Complete Breaths to create the right atmosphere of peace and tranquillity throughout the mind and the body. Though I have concentrated on the physical aspect of Yoga in this book, as I said in the beginning, it is impossible to divorce the body from the mind and all Yoga exercises, breathing or otherwise, must always affect all parts of the organism, both physical, mental, and spiritual.

When you have been practising Sun and Moon breathing for a few days and have established some sort of rhythm and balance in your performance, proceed to the next stage, which is the regulation of the length of your exhalations to twice that of your inhalations. Thus if you inhale to a count of four, then you exhale to a count of eight. I use four only as an example for the length of your inhalation must always depend on your individual capacity and comfort. I reiterate the warning about undue strain. Please, no straining in this or any other Yoga exercise. It can only do harm and achieve nothing.

After a few days of the above controlled breathing your next step is to prolong very gradually the retention of the breath until it equals the length of your inhalation. Thus if you inhale on a count of four then hold your breath for four and then exhale on a count of eight. Again you must adjust this counting to suit your own capacity.

This is the simplest form of Sun and Moon breathing and will suffice for our purposes in this chapter which deals with the calming of the mind and nerves. The advanced forms of this exercise call for almost superhuman discipline and are practised in connexion with the awakening of a mysterious force in the body known as Kundalini, the Serpent Power. This may briefly be described as the Divine Power of Knowledge and Wisdom from which, through civilization, Man has become separated. But the Kundalini, said to lie coiled at the base of the spine, is not dead but dormant, which is why every man is potentially divine no matter how far he may have strayed from the Divine Path.

But to return to your frayed nerves and wayward emotions, I will end this chapter with two simple exercises, one which combines breathing and movement and one which calms the mind and quenches thirst. The first of these is called THE L BALANCE STRETCH because while performing it your body roughly resembles the letter L.

1. Stand up straight, feet together and hands at your sides. Inhale deeply and at the same time raise your arms above your head, lace your fingers together and turn them palms upwards. Remain stretching upwards with your arms while you complete your inhalation.

2. Hold your breath for an instant and then, while exhaling slowly bend your knees until your calves are touching the backs of your thighs. Remain thus until you have completed your inhalation, with your arms still stretched above your head.

3. A natural pause will follow the completion of your inhalation, during which you should rise into the standing position and lower your hands to your sides.

When you can perform this exercise try a slightly more difficult version which requires you to hold the breath throughout the movement, thus:

1. Stand erect, inhale deeply while raising your hands above your head with the fingers laced as before.

2. When you have completed your inhalation hold your breath and bend your knees as before with your arms above your head. Remain in this position for as long as you comfortably can without exhaling.

3. When the impulse to exhale appears do so, at the same time rising to your feet. Repeat up to six times according to the time at your disposal.

This exercise taxes your sense of balance but it is a good exercise in calming the mind for it requires a considerable degree of concentration and muscular control to keep from over-balancing and this discipline, in conjunction with the deep slow breathing and the retention of the breath, results in a calm mind and soothed nerves.

In conclusion here is a simple exercise which imitates the respiration of the serpent. It is called *Sitali*, and it helps to calm the mind, purify the blood, quench thirst and cool the body when it is overheated. Protrude your tongue from your lips and fold it together to form a tube. Draw in the air through this 'tube' with a slight hissing sound until you have completely filled your lungs. Hold your breath for as long as you can and then exhale *through the nostrils*. SITALI should be practised up to twenty times a day. Combined with the other breathing exercises in this chapter the result will be a calmer, happier, more peaceful you.

CHAPTER FOUR

Insomnia, neurasthenia
and fatigue

IN the previous chapter I discussed emotional stress ailments. In this one we are considering the physical results of stress, worry, and constant fatigue. Perhaps the most common complaint of this modern age, together with constipation, which is discussed in the following chapter, is insomnia. It is the cause of more widespread misery than one could possibly imagine. There are many ways to combat insomnia but many people, far too many, rely on harmful and habit-forming sleeping drugs which may induce an unnatural sleep but which do not, and cannot, cure the trouble at the source. Indeed many people who have relied on them for years find that they are wholly unable to get a night's sleep without them. Yes, insomnia is one of the scourges of our time but Yoga has a way with it, nature's gentle and safe way.

The Yoga cure for insomnia and its dangerous resulting nervous exhaustion, is the natural one based on toning and relaxing the nerves, taking in more oxygen, and remaining immobile with the body inverted.

But first things first. What about the bed on which you sleep? Do you put up with just anything? Is it just a wooden frame, a mattress, and some pillows, sheets and blankets, or is it a supremely comfortable haven to which you can retire in blissful ease at the end of the day? No, I am not being fanciful. That bed on which you sleep may have more to do with your insomnia than you suspect. So let us consider it for a moment.

Have you sometimes suspected that your mattress was too soft and often wake up in the morning in a deep hollow with your mattress making 'water-wings' on either side of you? It is time, I fear, to think about replacing it with a firmer one.

34

Expensive? Perhaps, but after all you spend just about a third of your life in bed and if that third is plagued with insomnia due to an over-soft or worn out mattress is it not wise to consider spending a few dollars in order to improve your health, your spirits and your general well-being? Cheap at the price I would say.

And what about those mounds of bunchy pillows? Do these offenders grace your bed too? Send those packing with that soft mattress. It is essential in sleep that your spine should be held as naturally as possible. If you are lying in the hollow of a feather mattress with your head propped up on a mound of pillows, your poor spine is held in a highly unnatural position so if you do succeed in getting to sleep, which is often unlikely, you will be sure to wake up with morning backache, a stiff neck, a feeling of not having slept at all, and possibly a headache to add to the general confusion. If you suffer from any form of persistent backache one of the finest remedies I know, without doing another thing, is to buy a hard mattress. After you get used to sleeping on it you would never look a feather mattress in the face again. Sleep with as few pillows as possible, one small, firmly packed one is adequate for most people's needs. Why make your poor neck work hard while you are sleeping? What did it do to deserve that kind of punishment?

Next your clothing. It would seem unnecessary to mention this, but I am certain that far too many people wear too much clothing when they go to bed. Jumpers, cardigans, bed-jackets and socks are piled on over pyjamas and nighties, and heads are tied up in all kinds of scarves. But why? In winter why not one warm, cosy nighty or a pair of pyjamas, high necked and long sleeved, and in summer a wisp of nylon is all you need. Let your body b-r-e-a-t-h-e while you sleep. If you are cold add more blankets but do not, please, choke yourself to death.

It is often said that for most people the best sleep is before midnight. I do not necessarily agree with this and would gladly trade four hours of really deep natural sleep for eight hours of tossing, fitful dozing which for many people passes for sleep. You can easily work out for yourself how many hours of sleep you need in order to work at your maximum efficiency the next day. And do not make the common mistake of imagining you need more sleep than you actually do. Eight hours is what most people take to mean a good night's sleep but many people need only five or six, others need nine or ten. So make sure that you are not one of the former, as you may be getting your five or six hours of good sleep that you need and tossing about for the other two or three thinking that you suffer from insomnia. Do watch yourself carefully before you decide whether you need a cure for insomnia at all.

I find it restful to keep a book on my bedside table. No thrillers or ghost stories please. We are dealing with insomnia in this chapter and we cannot have you afraid to go to sleep being convinced that someone, or worst still SOMETHING has come to 'get you'. There is some controversy about plants and flowers being left in bedrooms overnight. My advice is to remove them if you can, for the carbon dioxide they give off at night will not help you one bit in this battle against your insomnia. Do sleep in a well-ventilated room with at least one window open, and if possible the door as well. A stuffy, overheated bedroom causes more headaches and insomnia than can be estimated.

Finally, place your bed so that you sleep with your head to the north and your feet to the south, or if this is absolutely impossible, sleep with your head to the south and your feet to the north. What you must avoid, you see, is sleeping across, instead of parallel to, the magnetic force lines of the earth. If again you accuse me of being fanciful, I can only tell you that I have known many people who have cured their insomnia, and its resulting stress ailments, simply by altering the position of their bed so that they lie parallel to the magnetic force lines of the earth. If you are sceptical (and you are a chronic insomniac) why not try it? You may be agreeably surprised.

Having disposed of the questions of how, when, and where you sleep, what you wear and what you lie on, I will now show you some Yoga exercises which will help you if you make careful note of all I have just said. Yoga will help you if you meet it half-way. Unlike some of the chapters in this book in which I have described Yoga asanas or postures which require patient practice, all the exercises in this chapter are very simple to do, with the possible exception of THE SHOULDERSTAND or Sarvangasana. This may be a little difficult for my older readers so let us try this one first.

1. Sit down on the floor with your spine straight and your legs stretched before you, ankles together. Roll backwards until your head touches the floor and your legs swing over your head.

2. Supporting your back with your two hands on either side of your spine, raise your legs to the vertical so that your toes are pointing towards the ceiling and your body is resting on the back of your head, the nape of your neck, and your shoulders. Press your chin against your chest in the chin lock. I have demonstrated the SHOULDERSTAND in figure 6, page 39.

Keep your body as straight as you can and hold yourself as still as possible. Resist the tendency to move your legs about in the air or to let your body sag at the waist. Close your eyes and breathe as deeply as you can. In the Shoulderstand breathing cannot be too deep but it should be as regular as your restricted lungs allow.

At first maintain the SHOULDERSTAND for only a few seconds but as you gradually become used to this inverted posture it can be held comfortably for several minutes. I suggest that you hold it for as long as you have the time but no more than ten to fifteen minutes. The main advantage of this valuable basic Yoga pose is that by holding the body inverted, in poised stillness, even for a few minutes, the thyroid glands are affected and so produce a powerful effect on the entire organism. Also the blood flows to the head by its own weight instead of it having to be pumped *upwards* by the heart so it not only gives the heart a respite from its ceaseless work but it also brings a flood of rich blood to the brain and so counteracts nervous fatigue, exhaustion, and other results of insomnia. But the benefits of the SHOULDERSTAND do not end there. Because it strengthens and tones the lower organs it is especially recommended for women after child-birth and those who suffer from menstrual pains.

A word of warning. If you suffer from any disorder of the thyroid gland or chronic sinusitis or nasal catarrh do not attempt to perform the Shoulderstand.

The adventurous among you might like to try a more advanced form of this posture, known as the SHOULDER BALANCE. In this the body is held as in the Shoulderstand but the support of the arms is removed. The arms are placed alongside the body and you are then balancing on your shoulders, neck and the back of your head and the extra effort you have to employ to maintain the body in this position with no support from your hands and arms generally intensifies the effect of the posture. You will not be able to hold the SHOULDER BALANCE as candle-straight as the Shoulderstand but do the best you can and above all hold yourself *still*. Keep your eyes closed and your chin locked against your chest.

Another variation of the SHOULDERSTAND, slightly more difficult but less tricky than the Shoulder Balance is to keep the arms and hands on the floor, either pointing the same way as your head or else extended at shoulder level, while the body is inverted. Again the extra effort required to keep the body straight and still without supporting the back intensifies the benefits of the posture.

One of the chief beneficial effects of the SHOULDERSTAND lies in the reversal of the influence of gravity on the internal organs. Few people appreciate how great this influence is. The body fluids tend to flow downwards and the skeleton is also subjected to constant downward displacement, and likewise the internal organs.

People with jobs that entail long hours of standing are most subject to varicose veins in the legs and prolapse of the viscera. In hospitals, patients suffering from these and allied ailments are placed on tilted beds so that the legs are higher than the feet. This practice, a modification of the Yoga asana I have just described, is to check the downward drag of gravity.

Nervous fatigue is due not only to emotional stress but also to the fact that the muscles of your back have to work long and hard just to hold you up. By inverting your body there is an immediate relief from this strain and the overtired feeling dissolves

FIGURE 6
SHOULDERSTAND

FIGURE 7
ROCKING EXERCISE

FIGURE 8
BACKBEND

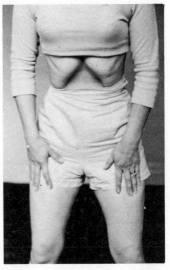

FIGURE 9
ABDOMINAL LIFT

into a pleasant feeling of relaxation. The SHOULDER-
STAND therefore is an invaluable exercise not only for insomnia
but for nervous fatigue, and tired or swollen legs.

As a prolonged Shoulderstand and, for some of my older
readers, even a brief one produces something of a strain and
tension in the neck, the following exercise known as Sethu
Bandhasana or the BRIDGE POSTURE will bring relief by
relaxing the neck and at the same time exercising the muscles
of the lower, middle, and upper back. It is fairly simple, if you
go carefully.

The Bridge Posture

From the Shoulderstand, and keeping your knees straight,
very slowly lower your legs until your feet are flat on the floor.
Do not lower your body from the waist upwards and keep your
hands supporting the back in the most comfortable position
which is usually on either side of the spine. Performed correctly
this exercise makes the body look like a graceful bridge. Hold it
for as long as you comfortably can and then slowly, very slowly,
lower your body and then your hands until you are lying flat.
Remain relaxed for a few minutes and take a few, deep recovery
breaths. The Shoulderstand should always be followed by the
Bridge Posture.

Although the Shoulderstand is one of the easier Yoga asanas
I am aware that many of my readers will be either too ill or too
stiff, or maybe even too overweight to perform this posture at
all. In that case you will obtain many, though not all, of the
benefits of the Shoulderstand by lying down on the floor in your
bedroom with your feet up on the bed. Practise the relaxation
exercise, Savasana, described in Chapter 2, with your feet above
your head. Hold your body still and relaxed and try to calm
your mind and clear away your mental and physical tensions. In
cases of fatigue and insomnia you will find this practice of
enormous help.

And now here is a very easy little ROCKING exercise which
will also help people suffering from insomnia. It can be performed
as a preliminary exercise to the Shoulderstand, as I will explain

presently, or else as an exercise just before you get into bed at night to help you sleep.

Rocking Exercises

1. Sit down on the floor, draw up your knees, and place your fingers behind your knees as in figure 7. Keep your head up and your back straight.

2. Let your body roll backwards until the back of your head touches the floor and your legs swing over your face. Keep your knees straight.

3. Rock yourself forwards again until you are in the starting position again.

Try this simple exercise a few times until you are able to control your movements. Remember to swing yourself back slowly so that your feet do not touch the floor behind your head. Use your hands to maintain your balance when you are perched on your seat and as your head goes down and your legs swing over. When you have gained some measure of control do the ROCKING EXERCISE as a slow and continuous movement, to and fro about a dozen times. You will find it very bracing and fatigue will soon disappear. Like so many other Yoga asanas it has the dual effect of producing energy in the body and at the same time calming the nerves. It is, therefore, beneficial both in cases of sleeplessness and of daytime fatigue.

Perform this exercise a dozen times and as you swing your legs over for the last time remove your hands from behind your knees and, supporting your back with them, rise into a SHOULDERSTAND. This is an excellent way of gathering momentum if you find it difficult to get into the Shoulderstand from the ordinary lying position. When you can perform the Rocking Exercise slowly and with absolute control, try then to match your breathing so that it is in rhythm with the to and fro movements of the exercise. All Yoga exercises should be accompanied by either Yoga deep breathing or rhythmic breathing.

Controlled breathing and stretching at the same time is the easiest method of quickly restoring freshness and vitality to a tired body. In particular the BACKWARD BEND calls into play not only the muscles of the back, torso and arms, but it also tones and refreshes the nerves, and taxes the sense of balance, therefore requiring a certain amount of concentration and discipline. There are many Yoga exercises which combine deep breathing with stretching and I will mention the most useful ones throughout this book. Here I choose the BACKWARD BEND for its particularly beneficial effects in the case of neurasthenia or nervous exhaustion.

Backward Bend

1. Stand with your feet wide apart and lace your fingers together and then turn them palms upwards. Slowly raise your arms above your head and at the same time bend backwards as far as you possibly can without overbalancing. I have demonstrated the correct movement in figure 8, page 41.

2. Remember to let your head go back as far as you can and turn your eyes upwards so that you are looking in the direction that your head is pointing. This is more beneficial than keeping them looking downwards, as it imparts a healthy exercise to the eyes.

3. Slowly return to the starting position and repeat *ad lib.* There is no special warning attached to the Backward Bend but if you have a hernia please go very carefully won't you. Bending backwards could do more harm than good in your case.

Do be careful not to overbalance as you lean backwards. This tendency can be avoided if you do not try to bend backwards to your utmost at first. Be content to go a little farther back each day you practise, and you will soon gain control in this valuable exercise.

And now for another breathing exercise which will restore vitality when you find you are at your lowest ebb. Those of you who have any difficulty in performing Yoga asanas, but nevertheless wish to study Yoga as a means of improving your general health can, with impunity, practise and perfect all Yoga breathing exercises. This one, to give you new zest and vitality, is called the NERVE RECHARGING BREATH. All Yoga breathing exercises are variations of the COMPLETE BREATH which I described in Chapter Three, and while I shall in this book describe several of the variations, I stress that they should be done in conjunction with the various asanas. In choosing the NERVE RECHARGING BREATH for this chapter on insomnia and neurasthenia I have borne in mind the fact that toning the nervous system and stretching the muscles and tendons is nature's own way of combating these two disorders which are so intrinsically linked together.

Nerve Recharging Breath

1. Stand up straight, legs apart, hands at your sides. While inhaling deeply raise your arms forward to shoulder height with your palms upwards. Complete your inhalation.

2. Close both your fists and, while holding your breath, pull your hands back slowly until your fists are resting against your shoulders.

3. When the impulse to exhale appears do so and at the same time slowly unclench your hands and lower them to the starting position. Repeat this exercise two or three times and then relax for a few moments before you perform any other exercise.

The Nerve Recharging Breath strengthens the nervous system and helps to overcome nervous trembling of the hands. It is also said to be helpful to people who lack self-confidence. Yoga is nothing if not all encompassing!

Practise in turn each of the exercises I have described in this chapter and after a surprisingly short time you will experience a new feeling of relaxation and freedom from stress, and when you get into bed at night you will surprise yourself by sinking into a profound and delicious sleep.

CHAPTER FIVE

Constipation and indigestion

THOSE who are masters of the science of Yoga refer to constipation as 'the mother of all diseases', and so many of the most important Yoga asanas aim at improving elimination and the digestive processes and, consequently, the health of the entire organism.

Among these exercises the ABDOMINAL LIFT is considered one of the most essential, not only for its physical values, but also for the way it influences our spiritual development by ridding the body, and therefore the mind, of impurities. Not only does the constant practice of it bring relief from chronic constipation and indigestion but it also strengthens flabby abdominal muscles and so improves the figure. But before attempting the ABDOMINAL LIFT it is advisable for beginners to spend the first two or three days limbering up the muscles with the following contracting and relaxing movements known as UDDIYANI.

1. Stand with the feet about twelve inches apart, inhale slowly and deeply and exhale with a good deal of force.

2. *Without inhaling again*, pull in the abdominal muscles with a strong upward movement until a hollow forms under the ribs. Hold for two seconds.

3. Relax the muscles, pull in again and relax again. Repeat this two or three times in quick successive movements, *still without inhaling*, and then relax.

Do not overdo these movements at first, and remember that the accent is on the pulling in movement rather than on the letting go.

Yoga exercises must be done while the stomach, bladder, and if possible the bowels are empty. First thing in the morning or last thing at night is convenient for most people but the time of day does not matter too much so long as the stomach is empty.

Allow at least four hours after a heavy meal, two hours after a light meal, and half an hour after a cup of tea or glass of fruit juice. Do not eat directly after exercising but wait at least half an hour. Be sure that nothing you wear fits tightly, or restricts your movement in any way.

After practising UDDIYANI for two or three days try the ABDOMINAL LIFT.

1. Stand feet apart, inhale deeply and use force to expel as much air from the lungs as possible.

2. Without inhaling again repeat the same upward and backward pull of the abdominal muscles as though trying to make as large a hollow as possible under the ribs. And this time *keep your muscles pulled in.*

3. Place your hands, palms down, on your thighs, bend your knees a little and then slightly tip your trunk forward but without lowering it. You will find that your diaphragm then rises easily. Do keep your hands pressed firmly against your thighs when leaning on them. I have demonstrated the correct position in figure 9, page 39.

4. Stay in this position for as long as you can without breathing and then relax. Repeat this exercise once more as it should not be overdone at first.

I reiterate the warning about strain, that there should be none whatsoever while performing this exercise. Muscular control can only be gained by *constant practice* and not by forcing flabby or rigid muscles into sudden, unaccustomed activity.

Very gradually increase the number of times you do this exercise, adding one ABDOMINAL LIFT each week until you are doing it seven times a day. At the same time try to increase the number of seconds you hold this position without breathing until you can hold it comfortably for ten seconds.

If, when you first attempt the Abdominal Lift you feel that ten seconds is an absolute impossibility, let me assure you that it can be done with perfect ease after careful practice.

Make sure that you are pulling in your abdominal muscles properly. You can either feel the hollow under your ribs with your hand or, better still, do the exercise in front of a mirror which has been tilted slightly backwards so that when you bend your trunk forward you will be able to see properly. Be sure not to bend your knees too much. And a word of *warning*. The Abdominal Lift should *not* be attempted by anyone suffering from heart, circulatory, or abdominal troubles.

If you find that the practice of UDDIYANI or the ABDOMINAL LIFT is too strenuous for you in a standing position, you may perform them sitting down in one of the classical poses described in Chapter 6, the Easy Pose or the Gupasana are recommended.

Chronic sufferers from constipation will benefit from the following internal cleansing method which is used by the Yogis. Internal purification is as important, if not more so, as external cleanliness. Take several glasses of water with a quarter of a teaspoon of salt per glass. The water must be at room temperature, *never* iced. Then do the contracting and relaxing movements (Uddiyani) while standing feet apart, then sitting on the floor with the spine straight and finally while lying flat on the floor. This is known as the 'avalanche technique' of taking an enema without any apparatus.

I have already discussed the importance of breathing in relation to health and each Yoga breathing exercise performs a different function in the body. Let us then consider a breathing exercise which will help to combat constipation and in addition will cleanse the lungs and the bronchial passages. It is called the BELLOWS BREATH or in Sanskrit, Bhastrika.

You have a choice of three positions for this exercise and you may adopt the one which you find most comfortable. You may either (A) sit down cross-legged on the floor, (B) sit on your heels, or (C) sit on a hard chair with your feet on the floor, close together. I need hardly say that whatever position you adopt the spine must be held erect. Not only in Yoga but always should the spine be straight whether you are sitting, standing or lying. Apart from your appearance, your health will improve as well.

Bellows Breath
   1. Sit down in your chosen position, rest your hands on your

thighs, and look straight ahead. First empty your lungs by bending your body forward to aid this action.

2. Take a deep slow breath through your nose and at the same time straighten your body gradually until you are in the starting position.

3. Complete your inhalation and as soon as your lungs are completely filled expel the air through your mouth with force, bending your body forward once again.

4. Without a pause the next intake of air follows at once and the whole process is repeated four times.

When you can perform the Bellows Breath four times without the slightest discomfort you may hold your breath for a few seconds every *fourth* intake of breath. When you can perform this exercise more than four times you know you are on the way to the breathing control which will be so beneficial to your health and spirits. I mention the word discomfort because if you are not used to deep breathing this, and indeed any other Yoga breathing exercise, might cause a slight dizziness which is a sure indication of how undernourished the blood is with oxygen. The dizziness will soon wear off but do not continue the exercise if any discomfort is felt. Lie down flat on the floor and close your eyes, leaving the exercise until the following day.

Increase the number of Bellows Breaths you take until you are performing the exercise twelve times, and remember to hold your breath after every fourth inhalation. This exercise stimulates the circulation of the blood, increases the flow of Prana or life-energy and, by increased oxygenization of the blood, the nerves are purified. And most important of all to sufferers from constipation, the bending forward and straightening up action of the exercise massages the internal organs and the viscera thus promoting digestion and evacuation.

Squatting Pose

This pose is exactly what its name implies. I want you to practise squatting like the people of the Orient do. They feel more comfortable in this simple position than they would sitting on a chair. You though may not, and especially at first, find it at all comfortable, but as an exercise for constipation it has few equals. The method is simple.

1. Stand up straight with your feet about twelve inches apart, inhale deeply and rise on your toes.

2. Complete your inhalation and begin to exhale immediately at the same time as you slowly bend your knees until you are sitting on your heels.

3. Hold the position for as long as you comfortably can and then, without inhaling slowly, rise to your feet. Then take a deep breath and repeat up to four times.

Practise this simple Squatting Pose for a few days and then try this slightly more difficult version. Proceed as above but this time do not raise your heels from the ground. Bend your body forward as you squat so that you do not overbalance, and bring your hands and arms forward over your knees so that your fingers touch the floor.

The third version of the squatting pose is even more difficult but with careful practice you will soon be able to do it. Proceed as for version 2 but this time keep your feet close together without raising your heels off the ground. You may wish to perform the three variations of this exercise and if so you should repeat each one twice. If you do only one, repeat it six times and do remember your breathing carefully.

If your knees are stiff or you are afraid of overbalancing you may steady yourself by holding on to a chair or anything convenient that will support your weight, until you feel more confident. After performing this exercise lie down on your back, stretch out your legs with your feet together, and relax for a few moments.

And now for an exercise which has an intriguing strangeness about it. It is called YOGAMUDRA and I have demonstrated it in figure 10. As you can see, it has an appearance of supplication about it and indeed, in the higher stages of Yoga the spiritual value of this asana cannot be over-emphasized. In some cases advanced Yogis hold this pose for an hour or more to help the awakening of the mysterious Kundalini or Serpent Power which I have already mentioned.

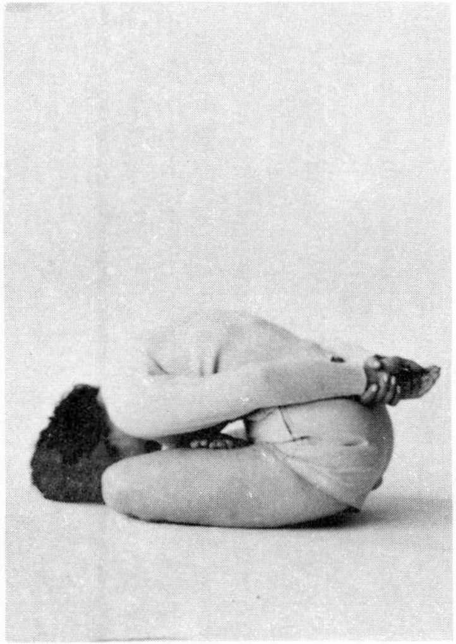

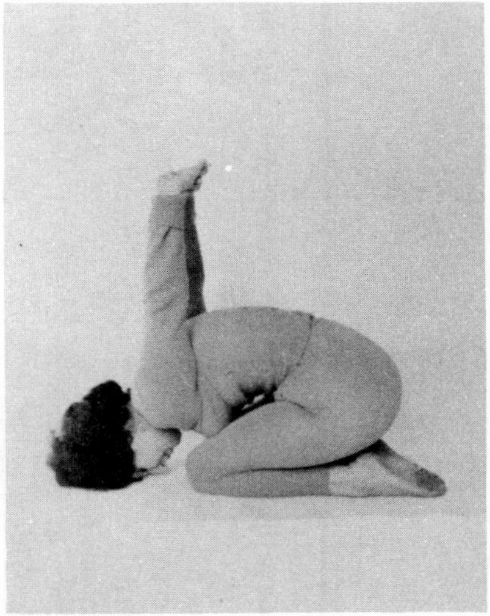

FIGURE 12 ARMSWING
BREATHING EXERCISE

FIGURE 11 HEAD TO KNEE
EXERCISE

FIGURE 10 YOGA MUDRA

49

But we are concerned, in this chapter, with constipation and YOGAMUDRA, by increasing the peristaltic movement of the bowel, promotes internal purification. It also tones and strengthens the abdominal muscles, the colon, and the pelvic region, and so it is a very valuable and health-giving posture indeed. There is an easy version for beginners but I will describe the classical one first.

1. Sit down in the Lotus Pose, which I have described in chapter six. With your hands behind your back clasp the right wrist with the left hand or vice versa.

2. Bend forward until your head touches the floor between your knees and remain so for as long as you find comfortable. When you are ready to straighten up do so very slowly and remain seated for a few moments with your back straight. You will experience a curiously light and peaceful sensation, as though you had just awakened from á peaceful dream.

But I can hear many of my readers protesting that the exercise I have just described is impossible. You can neither get into the Lotus Pose nor hope to reach the floor with your head. Very well, try this easier variation.

Sit down cross-legged on the floor, tailor fashion. This is the Easy Pose. Double your fists and place them firmly on either side of your navel. Now bend forward as before until your head touches the ground as near to your knees as you can. Your fists will impart a healthy massage to your abdominal organs just as, in the classical Yogamudra the upturned heels do likewise.

Yogamudra should be regarded not only as a powerful exercise to promote better elimination but also as an exercise in the calming of the mind. While your head is on the floor (and you will achieve this with patient practice) you should keep your eyes closed and try to empty your mind of all worries and fears. Practise repose and soon it will become a habit.

The following exercise should also be practised for the relief or prevention of constipation and/or indigestion. It should present little or no difficulty to the beginner, though perfecting it might take a little patience. Called the Janu Shirshasana or in English the HEAD TO KNEE POSE, it tones up sluggish bowels, strengthens the legs, and adds to your energy and vitality.

1. Sit down on the floor, both legs stretched out. Bend the left knee and place the left foot as high up as possible against the right thigh.

2. Inhale deeply, slightly raise your body from the waist upwards to pull in your stomach, and complete your inhalation.

3. While exhaling bend slowly forward and get hold of your extended right foot with both hands. The forehead should touch the right knee.

4. Remain in this position for as long as you comfortably can (which will be only a second or two at first) and then straighten up, at the same time straightening out your left leg. Repeat with the same leg and then change legs and repeat, twice bending your head towards the other knee.

For the ambitious among you, here is a slightly more difficult variation of this beneficial posture. Instead of placing your foot against the opposite thigh, place it *on* the thigh, afterwards bending the head towards the knee as before. I have demonstrated this position in figure 11, page 49.

At first many of you will find it difficult to reach your outstretched foot with your hands. This is because your spine has lost some of its flexibility or your abdomen (dare I whisper it) may have grown too large! Once you are limbered up you will find little difficulty and meanwhile I suggest you simply get hold of your calves, ankles or toes while bending your head towards your knee. If your knee appears to be an impossible distance away from your head I do assure you that with patient practice you will be able to do it with ease.

When you can perform the HEAD TO KNEE posture with ease you can graduate to a slightly more difficult variation in which the foot is placed on the thigh as above and the corresponding arm is placed right round the body to impart an extra pull to the muscles of the back, thus:

Variation of Head to Knee Posture

1. Sit down on the floor with your legs stretched out. Place

the right foot on the left thigh, as near to the body as possible.

2. Stretch forward your left hand and grasp the toes of your left foot.

3. Place your head on your left knee.

4. Keeping your head on your knee, reach your right arm round the back of your body and try to grasp the toes of your right foot which is on the left thigh. Remain thus for as long as you find comfortable, and without straining, and then straighten up, lie flat on the floor and relax, taking a few deep recovery breaths.

If you find you can do this variation you might like to omit the simpler Head to Knee posture in favour of this one, as the benefits of the asana are greatly enhanced by the added stretch to the muscles of the back and shoulders.

Yet another variation of the HEAD TO KNEE POSTURE requires a little more flexibility, and should not be attempted until you can perform the above variation with ease.

Variation of Head to Knee Posture

1. Sit down on the floor as before and place your right foot against your left thigh, as near to the body as possible.

2. Lift your left leg straight up and catch the foot firmly in both hands. Your leg should be perpendicular to the floor. Incline your head slightly until your face touches the knee of your raised leg. Hold this position for as long as you can and then repeat with the other leg. You may perform this variation up to six times, three for each leg. It will take time and patient practice to perfect, but it is well worth the extra effort as it will give an invigorating pull to the sciatic nerve as well as imparting the other benefits of the posture.

And now for something more spectacular. This is a colourful Yoga asana requiring flexibility and concentration. Called the Akarna Dhanurasana or in English the BOW AND ARROW POSTURE it will strengthen flabby abdominal muscles, thereby promoting better elimination, and will also limber up the joints of the hips, legs and shoulders.

Method

1. Sit down on the floor with your legs stretched out. Bend your right knee until your right foot is over your left thigh.

2. Grasp the right foot with the left hand to hold it in position while you

3. Raise your left elbow while drawing your right foot up to touch your left ear.

Your body now resembles a bow and drawn arrow. Look in the mirror while you perform it and you will see it is rather a dramatic-looking pose, deserving of its name, and certainly the benefits of it are dramatic too. Hold the pose for as long as you comfortably can and then return to the starting position. You may perform the BOW AND ARROW POSTURE up to four times, but please do not impart any strain to your muscles. You may hurt yourself and achieve nothing, so do go carefully.

Sufferers from both constipation and indigestion would do well to follow the water-drinking habits of the Yogis. Next to air, water is one of the bodily supplies most urgently demanded by nature. Eight-tenths of our physical body consists of water and about two quarts a day are eliminated. An insufficient intake of water is very often responsible for constipation, a congested colon, and malfunction of the liver and kidneys.

Drink a glass of fresh water, at room temperature, first thing in the morning and last thing at night. It should be taken hot only when your constipation is of long standing, or persistently troublesome, in which case unsweetened lime or lemon juice may be added to make it more palatable.

Water which has been boiled or processed often loses some of its vitality and to restore this pass it through the air, pouring it from one glass to the other, as this will prove more beneficial than drinking devitalized water.

Drink from six to eight glasses of water a day, or one glass for every fourteen pounds of your body weight. And remember that one of the greatest crimes in the black book of bad health is the drinking of iced water, or indeed any other iced beverage. Never, *never* drink anything straight from the refrigerator, no matter how pleasant you may think it is. Your health is more important than a few moments' pleasure don't you think?

Do not drink water with your meals but take it half an hour before or a couple of hours afterwards so as not to impair the digestive processes by diluting the digestive juices. One of the most powerful weapons against indigestion is the consideration of one's mental attitude while eating. Many people forget that the state of the body reflects the state of the mind and vice versa. So if food is eaten in a state of distress, anger or fear, it produces a toxic effect in the body and courts digestive troubles. And food improperly digested leads to chronic constipation and worse. It is far better not to eat if you are upset in any way, even though you might think that a good meal will make you feel better. Chances are it will not, and you will have a hefty attack of indigestion into the bargain.

It would seem unnecessary to mention that to swallow food in large, hurried mouthfuls first thing in the morning is not taking a good solid breakfast but cruelly treating the poor digestive system. By all means eat a good breakfast if you can take a lot of food in the morning, which many people can not, but do please eat it *sitting down*. If you bolt large quantities of food standing up with one eye on the clock you will spend half the morning trying to relieve yourself of the resulting digestive upset, and so lose that much working time. It is far better to take a little food, even a cup of tea with an egg and toast, and chew it slowly and calmly. Enjoy what you are eating and never eat anything you dislike because you think it is good for you. If you do not want it, you do not need it.

Unpleasant news should never be disclosed during, or just before, meals as this upsets the digestion and indeed the entire organism. A calm, methodical attitude towards life and its problems (which you will gain through the study of Yoga) will result in improved digestion, and better health and temper. Cultivate repose. It is the beginning of all Yoga, but it is not the body's and the mind's need alone. It is also the need of the world.

CHAPTER SIX

Backache and aching legs due to bad posture

HAVE we not often admired the graceful and dignified carriage of the average Indian man and woman, the coltish grace of their brown-limbed children? There is no magical secret to this natural grace, it is simply that in the East there are two natural sitting positions which are adopted from early childhood. One of these is cross-legged, whether in the so-called tailor fashion or with the soles upturned, in the classical Lotus Posture. The other is on the haunches with the feet flat on the floor. This 'squatting' pose is described in the previous chapter.

Americans complain that the cross-legged and squatting positions are unnatural and so they are—to those who are used to sitting on chairs. But in the East they are so accustomed to sitting like that that they actually find it more comfortable than any other position. Years of sitting in these positions tends automatically to hold the spine in a *naturally* erect position, not rigidly straight as some people seem to think, but held with its natural curves in the right place. And so, in walking the spine is also held naturally and gracefully and this is the simple 'secret' behind the superb carriage of the average Indian.

I do not for one moment expect the average American who reads this book to acquire the habit of sitting down in the Lotus Pose or even in one of the easier cross-legged poses. These positions should be included in the daily schedule of Yoga exercises and held for a limited time only unless you wish to proceed to the more contemplative forms of Yoga. The Lotus Posture, though graceful and serene in appearance is difficult and painful for the beginner and likewise the Half-Lotus position I have demonstrated on the cover.

However, there are three cross-legged poses which are not

beyond the reach of the more supple among you, though I warn you that even quite young people in their early twenties sometimes have knees so stiff that they cannot sit cross-legged on the floor. I will describe these seated postures in turn, beginning with the LOTUS POSITION and you can try them for yourself.

1. *Lotus Position*

The advantage of this position is that it forms a symmetrical and firm seat so that the Yogis, in states of deep spiritual trance, did not overbalance. Sit down on the floor with your legs stretched out, feet together. Take the right foot in both hands and place it high up on the left thigh. The right knee should be pressed firmly to the floor. Take the left foot in both hands and draw it gently over the bent right leg so that the left foot is placed on the right thigh. I have demonstrated the correct position in figure 14, page 57.

2. *Siddhasana* (Half-Lotus position)

If you are unable to master the Lotus position this one is considered by many to be somewhat easier, and at the same time more comfortable. Certainly it is preferred by many Yogis to the full Lotus Pose. (See figure 14.) Sit down as before and place one foot with the heel against the perineum. The other foot is then placed on the opposite thigh with the heel pressed against the pubic bone. The hands should be placed as in the Lotus Pose, with the thumb and first fingers joined and the palms upwards.

3. *Easy Pose*

Sit down on the floor, tailor fashion, with the heel of one foot touching the perineum and the heel of the other underneath the opposite ankle. This is considerably easier than either the Lotus or Half Lotus positions.

If you are very stiff and find all three of these positions agonizing, then please do not pursue the matter. I do not want you to suffer unnecessary pain, but if you think you possibly

FIGURE 14   LOTUS POSE

FIGURE 13   ACCOMPLISHED POSE

could master one or all of them then do try for the sake of your posture.

The last of the seated postures I will describe in this chapter is as follows:

Samasana or the Symmetrical Pose

Sit down on the floor and bend the right leg, placing the heel against the pubic bone and resting against the left thigh. Bend the left leg and place the foot over the right one so that the heel is set against the pubic bone and the toes are pushed between the right thigh and calf. People who cannot master the other three seated postures I have described are often able to sit down in Samasana without difficulty or discomfort. (See Fig. 13.) All three positions will hold the spine in a naturally erect position and so promote better posture.

The effective functioning of the entire organism is closely linked to the healthy condition of the spinal column and cord. As your body grows older there is a tendency for the vertebrae to become rigid especially after a lifetime of abuse in the form of bad sitting, walking or standing. If the body is habitually held in postures which involve slouching the spinal column tends to get out of alignment. In discussing this problem of backache we must face the fact that much of it is due to bad posture. Cure the one and the other disappears, and automatically there is an improvement in the general health and well-being.

I must warn you before I go any farther that a few days practice of the asanas I will describe in this chapter will not eliminate the effects of years of bad posture. If you would cure your backache, your round shoulders, and your rather ungraceful carriage you will have to work at it. You must keep a wary eye open at all times to see if you are slouching. People who work at typewriters are among the worst offenders here. Do sit with the base of your spine firmly against the back of your chair so that the back of it supports the lower back. Sit erect at all times and soon it will become a healthy habit.

The following simple exercise will help to limber up the spine and prepare it for more difficult postures. It is easy and bracing and is a vital first blow in our battle against bad posture. Similar to the Rocking exercise described in chapter four. Try this when you get out of bed in the morning.

The Half Somersault

1. Sit down cross-legged and grasp your toes with your arms outside your knees.

2. Bend forward and try to touch the floor with your forehead. No? Well bend forward as far as you can.

3. Still holding your toes straighten your back and at the same time inhale deeply through the nose.

4. Hold your breath for a moment and then bend forward again while exhaling and when your lungs are empty roll backwards keeping your chin pressed firmly down into your chest in the chinlock I have mentioned before.

5. Roll forwards once more while inhaling until your spine is straight. Hold this position while you complete your inhalation.

6. While exhaling through your mouth bend forward once more to the starting position.

And that is all. Very easy this one, but two points to remember. The whole exercise should be performed slowly and rhythmically, with nasal inhalations and oral exhalations. It is best performed with the eyes closed which is very calming to the mind and nerves. The benefits are many but principally the Half Somersault brings into play the muscles of the back, toning and stretching the whole of the spinal column.

The YOGAMUDRA exercise I described in the previous chapter is also beneficial to people with backache and bad posture.

Many of the Yoga exercises are based on the natural stretching of healthy animals which the ancient Yogis, who formulated the science of Hatha Yoga, observed and emulated. Therefore, many Yoga asanas are named after mammals, birds, sea creatures, insects, and reptiles. In this chapter we meet the Swan and the Camel.

The Swan Posture (Swanasana)

As its name indicates, it is a graceful exercise and will, therefore, especially appeal to women readers, although its benefits also to male sufferers from backache can hardly be over-estimated. Like many other Yoga asanas the Swan Posture consists of two opposite movements which I have demonstrated in figures 15 and 16, page 61.

1. Lie face downwards, feet together, palms flat on the floor at the level of your armpits. Keep your elbows well off the floor. While inhaling deeply through the nose, and pressing downwards on the floor with your palms, slowly raise your head, shoulders and abdomen off the floor until your elbows are straight. (Fig. 16.)

2. Remain in this position for as long as you comfortably can while holding your breath.

3. While exhaling, and keeping your palms firmly on the floor *without moving them* slowly raise your abdomen, bend your knees, and sink into the kneeling position I have demonstrated in figure 15. Keep your forehead on the floor, your thighs pressed against your abdomen, and your buttocks on your heels. Remain thus while holding your breath.

4. When the impulse to inhale again appears do so and at the same time raise your buttocks off your heels, straighten your knees and, still without moving your palms return to the starting position as in figure 16.

5. Repeat this to and fro movement up to six times and do be careful to perform your breathing correctly.

And that is the Swan exercise. Graceful and beneficial, it massages and helps to reduce the abdomen in the kneeling movement and the other movement helps relieve backache and improves the posture. The to and fro movement combats constipation and promotes the peristaltic movement of the bowel.

The Camel Posture (Ustrasana)

This is another Yoga exercise which involves a backward bend. I warn you before you attempt this exercise that it is not as easy as it looks, and great care must be taken while coming out of this position. As in all Yoga asanas you must take your time and move without jerking and in particular this applies to movements involving the spinal column. *The Camel* is simple enough.

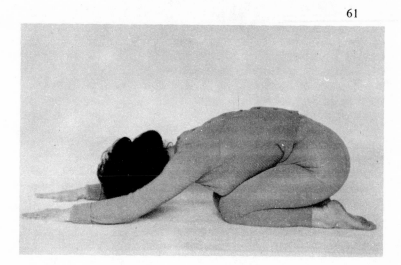

15

FIGURES 15, 16   SWAN POSTURE

16

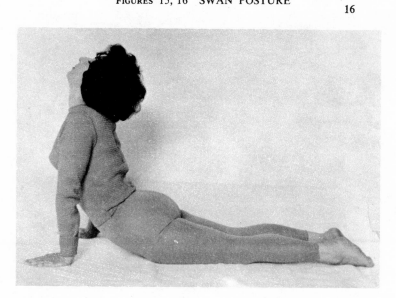

FIGURE 17   CAMEL POSTURE

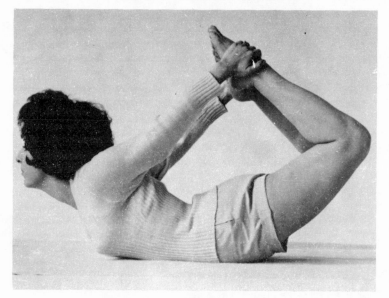

FIGURE 18   BOW POSTURE

1. Kneel down and sit back on your heels with your toes outstretched.

2. Place your hands on the floor palms down, just behind your toes. Your fingers should be pointing away from your body.

3. Lean on your hands, throw back your head, and while inhaling very slowly lift your buttocks off your knees until your spine is fully arched. I have demonstrated the correct Camel Posture in figure 17, page 62.

4. Remain in this position for as long as you comfortably can while holding your breath then very slowly and carefully lower your body until you have returned to the starting position. It is during this part of the exercise that you have to take the greatest care as there is great strain on the back of the neck and if you jerk back to the starting position you could get a nasty rick in your neck.

So please go carefully and you will greatly benefit from this valuable posture. It tones and strengthens the muscles of the spine and gives it greater elasticity. It will also correct any displacements in the vertebrae and will strengthen the neck and shoulders. *A word of warning*. The Camel Posture should not be attempted by anyone suffering from hernia or serious abdominal disorders.

In writing this chapter on backache and bad posture I have not forgotten the many people who suffer from sacroiliac troubles. Here is a Yoga exercise which will bring relief from this tiring and distressing complaint.

The Centred Spine Bend

1. Stand up straight, feet together and your hands at your sides. Cross your left foot over your right with the toes of your left foot on the floor and the heel off. Your right knee-cap should lie behind the back of the left knee. Resist the temptation to move your body to the left as it is important that your spine should remain centred, and do not try to straighten your knee.

2. Inhale deeply through the nose and while exhaling bend forward, very slowly and carefully, until your finger tips touch

the floor or if you are very stiff bring your fingertips as near to the floor as you can. Do not try to force your hands lower than they will comfortably go. With constant practice you will be able to reach the floor when you will obtain the maximum benefit from this exercise.

3. Remain in the bending position for as long as you comfortably can without inhaling. When the impulse to inhale appears do so and at the same time straighten up again.

4. Repeat the CENTRED SPINE BEND three or four times then reverse legs and repeat thus three or four times. Two points to note. Firstly do not move your shoulders or your buttocks while bending forward, as all the work should be done by the spine above the waistline. If you perform this exercise very slowly and carefully and practise it faithfully at least three or four times a day you will soon experience relief from your sacroiliac troubles.

The next Yoga asana in this chapter is the BOW POSTURE (Dhanurasana) which is an intensification of another asana named the Cobra which you will meet in chapter twelve. Dhanurasana is so named because it strongly resembles an archer's bow and is, you will agree, a very beautiful posture and incidentally is a powerful weapon in our war against backache for the vertebrae are moved in such a way that the nerve ganglions receive a richer supply of blood.

It also exerts a healthy pressure on the kidneys, thereby correcting any disorders in their function.

Bow Posture

1. Lie face downwards on the floor, hands along your sides and feet together.

2. Inhale deeply and bend your legs keeping them as close together as possible. Stretch your arms upwards and backwards and grasp your ankles.

3. Pull your legs as high off the floor as you possibly can by fully arching your spine. Hold this position for as long as you comfortably can while holding your breath.

4. When the impulse to exhale appears do so and slowly

return to the starting position. I have demonstrated the correct position in figure 18, and you can see why this posture is named the BOW.

At first you will be able to hold this posture for only a few seconds but very gradually extend this period until you can hold it for a full minute. You may perform it up to six times a day, but no straining though.

I foresee that many of you will have some little difficulty with this asana. Either you will not be able to keep your knees together or worse, you may not be able to raise your legs off the floor at all. In this case try this easier method. Pull one leg up at a time and you will soon find that your muscles will be stretched and limbered up and you will be able to bend your body into a perfect and beautiful Bow.

This is a wonderful exercise for the relief of backache but as it is rather a strenuous posture do please practise it carefully.

The Bow Posture may be preceded by the *Stomach Balance* which is the very simplest of the backward bending exercises for the relief of backache.

1. Lie face downwards with your arms extended in front of you, palms downward.

2. While inhaling deeply slowly raise your arms and legs off the floor so that you are balancing on your abdomen. Bring your head up as high as you can.

The higher you can raise your head and legs the more effective is the Stomach Balance. Hold the position for as long as you can without exhaling and then, as the impulse to exhale appears slowly return to the starting position. Though a simple exercise it needs care as all the backward bends tend to be somewhat strenuous. The Stomach Balance tones up the entire nervous system and stretches the muscles of the back and abdomen.

The Bow Posture being one of the most beautiful of the Yoga asanas it will appeal especially to women and here is a variation which is also striking in its aesthetic appeal. It looks like the graceful swimming of some exotic fish, and on a more practical level let me assure you that it is considerably easier than the full BOW POSTURE which I have just described.

Variation of the Bow Posture

In this variation half the body is kept straight and half bends backwards. Lie face downwards, bend the right knee and catch the toes of the foot with your right hand. Slowly pull the foot towards your head bending only the muscles on the right side of the back. The left arm should be held outstretched and the left foot likewise. Seen from the side this posture has all the grace of the lovely BOW and something else all its own.

And now here is another breathing exercise which will help to counteract bad posture, drooping and round shoulders, and curvature of the spine. It also improves flabby upper arms, and excessive flesh on the shoulders will slowly be squeezed away. It is called the ARMSWING BREATHING EXERCISE.

1. Sit back on your heels with your spine straight. Lace your fingers together and then turn them palms upwards.

2. Inhale deeply and at the same time bend forward until your chin is touching the floor as in figure 12, page 49.

Swing your arms upwards as high as you possibly can trying again and again to swing them just a little higher. Hold this position for as long as you can without exhaling. When the impulse to exhale appears do so as you straighten up again. Relax and repeat from four to six times, after which lie down for a few moments and take a few deep recovery breaths.

If your knees are very stiff or if for some other reason you are unable to sit on your heels you may perform the Armswing Breathing Exercise standing up in which case you lean forward from your waist as far as you can and bring your arms with the fingers interlaced, as far forward as you can. The movement from the waist will help to remove fatty tissue in this area and help the spine towards a new suppleness.

The warning not to jerk any movements is reiterated here as you should not try to swing your arms over violently as you may well injure a rigid muscle which would discourage you from ever attempting this valuable exercise again. Nothing is more painful than a muscle spasm. Practise this exercise every day and you will soon notice a marked improvement in your posture and a new feeling of freedom from backache and a new feeling of lightness as your straightening spine allows your lungs to take in more oxygen. All parts of the body are interdependent. Cure your backache and your chest complaints are eased, your temper improved, and your looks enhanced. Do not under-estimate the gravity of bad posture. It may not be an illness but it has a well-deserved place in this book on Yoga and health because it can, ultimately, undermine the health of the entire organism by restricting breathing, and cause an unhealthy complexion due to too little oxygen reaching the blood cells. Attack your bad posture and its resulting backache like the enemies they are.

Many people suffer from bad posture and an ungraceful carriage because of weak legs, ankles, or feet. The remainder of this chapter is devoted to the consideration of these particular conditions and I will explain how they can be greatly helped by Yoga's methods. It has often been said that a man's temper is only as good as his feet. If the feet ache and burn how is it possible to be smiling and at ease? If your legs hurt or are swollen with varicose veins how easy it is to snap at everyone and feel that the world is a terrible place.

In this book on health I must always be on guard against anything which can disrupt the dawning calmness of the mind which my readers must experience if they have been faithfully putting into practice all I have written about so far. In practising relaxation you will have discovered a new peace with yourself. In practising the breathing exercises you will feel a new glow of vitality. And if you have practised the asanas your health will have begun to improve beyond your wildest hopes, and with it you will have discovered a new lease of life within yourself, a zest for living, a new inner power. So we cannot let tired, swollen and aching feet hold up the new feeling of health and freedom opening out before you. We cannot let them undo all your good work. So start by putting them up higher than your head whenever possible. It isn't done in the so-called best of circles to put your feet on the mantelpiece. Never mind about that. Yoga dosen't know any class barriers. Go on, put them up, it will do them good. And before going out in the evening nothing could be more restful than lying on the floor in your bedroom and putting your feet up on the bed. Remain like that for a few moments with your eyes closed and you are a new man—or woman. The change is remarkable. You are refreshed and alive and your legs and feet no longer feel like lead.

The following breathing exercise added to your daily asanas will help to strengthen weak ankles, improve flabby calves, and soothe painful or fallen arches.

The Arched Foot Breathing Exercise

1. Stand erect, with your hands on your hips. While inhaling slowly and deeply hook your left foot round the back of your right foot with the toes pressing against the ankle of your right foot.

2. At the same time rise up on the toes of your right foot and remain balanced in this position while you complete your inhalation, and hold your breath for as long as you can.

3. When the impulse to exhale appears do so and at the same time slowly lower your right heel to the floor and unhook your left foot. Both heels should reach the floor at the same time.

4. Repeat this exercise with the legs reversed.

The Arched Foot Breathing Exercise taxes your sense of balance but as in all such exercises it can be used as a valuable exercise in concentration. You will wobble about at first but gradually you will be able to remain balanced on the toes of one foot with your hands on your hips, and remain so for as long as your breath allows you. The practice of this exercise will not only improve your balance but fine down calves and ankles that may be a little too heavy for your liking.

Any exercise which tones and stretches the leg muscles and the sciatic nerve will bring relief from aching legs and so do not omit from your daily practice schedule the exercises described in the following chapter on lumbago and sciatica. And if you suffer from that most distressing and common complaint, varicose veins, nothing could be more helpful than the habitual practice of the Shoulderstand which I described in chapter four. Also do not omit the simple, leg stretching exercise described in chapter two. Remember the basic principle regarding the relief of aching legs and feet. Put them up higher than your head for in this position your legs are not subject to the downward pull of gravity and are therefore being rested. As you lie there with your feet higher than your head try to calm your mind and still your thoughts so that this period of rest becomes a powerful exercise in mind control and mental stillness.

As a general rule people who study and practise Yoga do not worry overmuch about their looks, in fact they have a natural beauty of face and figure which comes from pure living and mental serenity. But if you suffer from bad feet and aching legs, as your condition gives way under Yoga's gentle persuasion, you will find that your looks will improve in a surprising way. Those wrinkles of pain, tiredness and discomfort are soon ironed away from your brow and around your eyes and your general well-being cannot but be affected by the improvement of your means of getting about from place to place. It is a constant source of concern to me that so many people neglect their legs and feet yet spend dollars and valuable time on their hair and their clothes. If you want all to be well with your world get to work now on those bad feet of yours and remember the old and wise saying, "A man's temper is only as good as his feet'!

CHAPTER SEVEN

Lumbago and sciatica

IN the previous chapter I discussed backache and aching legs due to bad posture and long hours of standing. The antidote was based on limbering up the spine and keeping it supple, bending it this way and that to relieve tired muscles, and putting the feet up above the head to combat the pull and downward drag of gravity. The antidote in this chapter is based on toning up the sciatic nerve and the muscles of the lower back to relieve the pain of sciatica and lumbago.

The first Yoga asana I would like you to try combines the two processes. I warn you it is not one of the easier ones but because of its value you should persevere and try to master it. Yoga is a perpetual challenge for thinking people. Anything easily gained is lightly prized, so when you have mastered THE FORWARD BEND or PASCHIMOTTANASANA you will feel that you have really achieved something. As usual I will describe the easiest variation first.

Forward Bend

1. Lie flat on your back, hands at your sides and feet together. Keeping your legs straight and your heels on the floor slowly raise your trunk from the waist until you are in a sitting position.

2. Stretch out your arms, bend forward, and grasp your toes with your fingers. If you cannot reach your toes grasp your calves or ankles until you have limbered up your spine enough to be able to bend it more fully and reach your toes easily.

3. Bring your forehead down until you can press it against your knees. Did I hear you say 'impossible'. Most people say that but if you take a quick look at figure 20 you will see that it is not only entirely possible but actually rather easy when you can once do it. But your spine is too stiff at the moment is it not, to perform this kind of bending so be content, at this stage, to

bring your forehead as close to your knees as you can even if this means only a slight inclination of your head. If you proceed slowly and gently you will find that your spine will graudally loosen up, your head will be able to go lower, and soon you will be able to press your face to your knees.

4. Remain in this position for as long as you comfortably can and then very slowly bring your arms down to your sides, straighten up, and lower your body to the floor again until you are in the starting position. Lie there and relax for a few moments and attempt the Paschimottanasana only once more. Twice a day is enough at first. As you gradually become used to this exercise try to extend the period when your head is on your knees in which case you need only perform this asana once.

Once you get used to the Forward Bend and can do it tolerably well, proceed as follows which incorporates the Yoga breathing as well.

1. Lie flat, take a deep breath, and at the same time sit up.

2. While exhaling bend forward and grasp your toes, ankles, or calves. (Fig. 19, page 73.)

3. Bring your forehead on to your knees without inhaling again. The extreme bend will force all the air out of your lungs. Lower your elbows to the floor as in figure 20 and remain thus for as long as you can without breathing.

4. When the impulse to inhale appears do so while straightening up slowly.

5. When you have completed your inhalation slowly lie down until you are in the starting position. Remain relaxed for a few moments and take a few deep recovery breaths.

This exercise is a more advanced form of the Head to Knee exercise which I described in chapter five. If you can perform the Head to Knee successfully the Forward Bend will not give you too much difficulty. Its benefits are many. It gives the maximum of bending capacity to the body and at the same time imparts a stimulating pressure on the viscera. In stretching the spinal column to the greatest degree it helps to relieve and prevent sciatica and lumbago. Like the Head to Knee posture it tones up sluggish bowels and helps to promote better elimination, thereby being a cleansing and purifying exercise which will help to rid the body of the impurities which cause pain and disease. For this reason it is practised in the higher stages of Yoga for its spiritual values for spiritual purity is closely linked to physical purity.

There is a standing variation of the Forward Bend which some of you might like to try. It is possibly slightly more difficult for the beginner as the support of the floor is removed from the legs but the value of the posture is greatly enhanced by the extra effort involved.

1. Stand up straight with your hands at your sides. Inhale deeply, slowly raise your arms above your head but without joining your fingers. Remain thus until you have completed your inhalation.

2. While exhaling bend forward from the waist and place your palms just below your calves.

3. As you complete your exhalation press your head against your knees as I have demonstrated in figure 35. Remain thus until the impulse to inhale appears.

4. Straighten up as you inhale, and complete your inhalation with your spine erect and your hands at your side. Perform this asana only once or twice at first and do not under any circumstances try to force your muscles in any way. The FORWARD BEND is one of the Yoga exercises which helps to keep old age at bay. Many Yogis live to be well over a hundred years old yet still look young and remain active. When asked their secret they will tell you, 'A man is only as old as his spine'. Keep this saying in mind and vow to remain supple and active for ALL of your life and not just for a third of it!

Before we leave the FORWARD BEND I would like to describe the advanced form of it used by really enthusiastic students. They do not catch the toes with their fingers, instead they rest their forearms *on* the toes with the elbows straight. The hands are held palm to palm, and the head is then pressed to the knees as before.

Advanced students, or the more supple among you, might like to try another forward bending exercise which brings the maximum flexibility to the lumbar region and its ligaments. It is

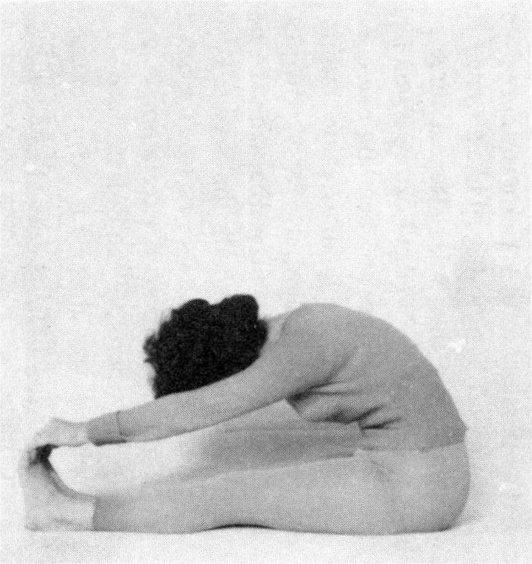

FIGURES 19, 20   BENDING FORWARD

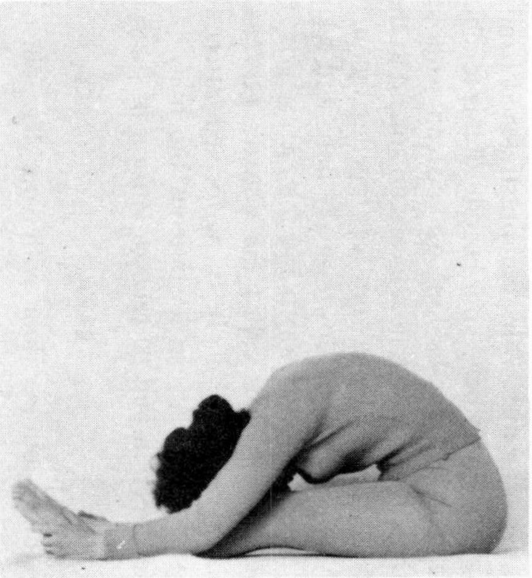

called Oopavishta-Konasana, or in English the PRISM POSTURE.

1. Sit down on the floor with your legs outstretched. While inhaling deeply move your legs as wide apart as possible.

2. Catch your toes with your outstretched hands and while exhaling very slowly bend your head until it is touching the floor.

3. Remain thus for as long as you can without breathing. When the impulse to inhale appears do so and at the same time raise your head and bring your legs together again.

After this exercise lie down on the floor and relax.

After the FORWARD BEND and the PRISM POSTURE, here is something easier. It is called the WEDGE POSTURE and it is particularly beneficial if it is performed after any forward bending exercise because it stretches the body in exactly the opposite direction and so relieves tension in the muscles.

Wedge Posture

1. Sit down on the floor with your legs outstretched, feet together. Place your hands behind you, palms down, and your fingers pointing away from your body.

2. Adjust the position of your hands according to your personal build and capabilities and then raise your body, keeping it as straight as possible until you are resting on your heels and your hands. Your body is now shaped like a wedge. Remain as this for a few seconds, and then relax. Repeat three or four times. Remember to perform the Wedge Posture if you feel any tension in your muscles after a forward bending exercise. It stretches, limbers, and strengthens the lumbar region and its ligaments.

And now here is something new for you to try if you have sciatica. Tone up your sciatic nerve first with the Forward Bend, loosen those knotted muscles with the Wedge Posture and then sit down to do the GOMUKASANA or BULL POSTURE.

Many Yoga asanas are named after animals and it is usually easy to see why, but wherefore the Bull posture? If you will look at figure 23 perhaps it will explain. My feet are arranged on either side of me rather like the horns of a bull don't you think? This Sanskrit name is sometimes translated as Cow-Face Posture, but I feel that aesthetically it is all wrong to give this rather graceful posture such a name. Still names are not that important. What matters is to relieve your sciatica, so let us begin.

Bull Posture

1. Sit down on the floor, spine straight and legs outstretched. Bend your right leg and place it over the left one with your right heel against your left hip.

2. Bend your left leg and place your left heel against your right hip. You are now in the position I am demonstrating in figure 23 with your right leg uppermost.

3. Hold this position for as long as you comfortably can and then change over your legs so that your left is uppermost.

You will feel the stretch imparted to the sciatic nerve in the leg which is uppermost. If your sciatica is very painful I hope you will not try to force your legs where they will not easily go as this would cause you a great deal of pain and discomfort. Slowly and gently is the word here, practise a little each day and you will soon be able to execute a beautiful Bull posture. If any part of your leg or hip aches when you attempt this asana this can be strongly massaged with your fingers to bring relief. If you proceed with *extreme* caution this asana, more than any other with the possible exception of the Forward Bend, will loosen the sciatic nerve and restore elasticity.

If you do not suffer from sciatica regular practice of the Bull Posture will ensure that you never do. Your muscles in the lower half of the back will be strengthened so sufferers from lumbago will also find the Bull Posture of great value. When, after careful practice, you can perform this asana to your liking and can hold it in comfort for several minutes, while you hold it practise deep breathing with your eyes closed and your spine held straight. You will find it a valuable exercise in the calming of the mind, and this calmness should be reflected in the serene expression of the face.

The next stage of the Bull Posture involves the arms and shoulders. As you sit comfortably in this seated posture raise the hand corresponding to your leg which is uppermost and bring

it behind your shoulder. At the same time bend the other arm
backwards and upwards and join your fingers together. Proper
execution of this movement will develop your trapezoidal
muscles, and prevent bursitis, and arthritis of the shoulders.
It may take a little practice for you to be able to join your
hands together in this novel way but do go slowly and you will
soon succeed. It is well worth a little effort.

The Squatting Pose which I described in chapter five will also
bring relief to sufferers from lumbago and sciatica. Though not
a beautiful posture it is an invaluable one. Yoga, as a general
rule, is as graceful as ballet dancing in its static grace as opposed
to the fleeting movements of ballet, but the ancient Yogis in
their wisdom did not omit several ungraceful postures for the
sake of the body's health and well being. Such a one is the
Squatting Pose and there are several others scattered about in
these pages. They are included for a very good reason so do not
omit them because of their lack of aesthetic appeal.

But now, to make up for the ungainly Squat which will greatly
help your lumbago and sciatica here is an equally beneficial
one which has all the bizarre grace of the insect from which it
takes its name.

Salabhasana or the Locust Posture

1. Lie face downwards, chin touching the floor, hands along
your sides, palms either clenched or flat on the floor.

2. While inhaling deeply raise your right leg as high as you
possibly can, pressing into the ground with your clenched fists
or flattened palms to give yourself more leverage. I have demonstrated the correct position in figure 22, page 77.

3. Hold this position as you complete your inhalation and
then slowly lower your leg as you exhale. Repeat with the other
leg. Keep the raised leg as straight as you can and perform this
asana six times in all, three times with each leg.

When you have practised with alternate legs for a few days
try the full Locust Posture which involves the raising of both legs
simultaneously as in figure 21. This variation of the Locust
Posture is much more difficult but the added effort involved

FIGURE 21   LOCUST POSE (FULL)

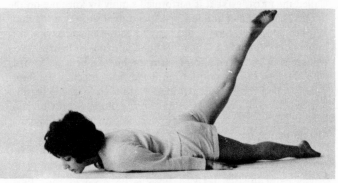

FIGURE 22   LOCUST POSE (HALF)

FIGURE 23   BULL POSTURE

77

greatly enhances the benefits of this valuable posture. It has the added benefit of toning and strengthening the muscles and organs of the abdomen as well as bringing relief from our two antagonists of this chapter.

When you can perform the full Locust Posture hold it for as long as you comfortably can while holding your breath. Repeat up to six times a day.

The next posture I would like you to try is deceptively simple. Called the FROG POSE it is performed simply by kneeling on the floor, knees together and feet apart, and then sitting on the floor between your feet. Simple did I say? I can hear you saying it is impossible. Not only is it possible but if you look at figure 53 you will see it in its extreme form when the body is bent backwards with the legs in this position until the head touches the floor. This is called the Kneeling Bridge Posture so if this is feasible how much more easy is the simple Frog Pose. So do practise it and your sciatica will gradually succumb to its nerve tugging, muscle toning persuasion.

I would like to refer you once again to chapter five in which I have described the Yogamudra. This exercise has very many benefits and not the least of these is its effect on the spinal column and the muscles on either side of it. For the relief of lumbago you would do well to practise it until you can perform it to perfection and hold it for some time. Remember to do deep Yoga breathing while in this position and straighten up as soon as you begin to feel the slightest strain. In the two complaints with which this chapter is concerned it is of vital importance that you do not strain any nerve or muscle. Once again I reiterate the words 'slowly and gently'.

I cannot mention the Yogamudra twice in this book without telling you of the spiritual values it confers. Although we are primarily concerned in this book with improving the health let us never forget that the practice of Hatha Yoga cannot but have a beneficial effect on the mind and spirit. Yogamudra, one of the basic Yoga asanas, is essentially a cleansing exercise, both of the system and of the mind. Students in the advanced stages of Yoga remain in this position for as long as an hour or more.

I am not asking you to attempt such a feat of endurance but I would like you to experience the effects of just a few quiet moments spent in sitting in this posture, when you can do it, that is. I am aware that for some of you this will take some time. But as you straighten up you will experience a new clarity of vision, a new awareness, and a heigthened sense of power and well-being. You will, as you come to learn more and more Yoga asanas, adopt your own particular favourites and I have heard from many people that Yogamudra is one of the most popular Yoga asanas. Not an easy one but how worthy it is of your time, your patience and your endeavour.

And now to end this chapter I will describe one of the most beautiful and dramatic postures in the entire Yoga range. Strikingly graceful, it is worthy of a place in the most classical of ballets. Called ANJANEYASANA or in English the WING POSTURE it makes the human body into a living poem of static grace and at the same time limbers up the muscles of the lower back, the thighs, and the shoulders. But as it is one of the most beautiful so it is one of the most difficult to perform perfectly, though beginners will be able to perform it in a modified way with little difficulty. I include it in this book because it is far too beautiful to be left out, and also because to sufferers from lumbago and sciatica it is of great and lasting benefit.

Anjaneyasana or the Wing Posture

1. Kneel down with your feet together. Your body should be straight from the knees upwards. Place your right foot on the floor so that the upper leg is at right angles to the lower leg. Stretch your left leg back as far as possible, keeping the knee on the ground. Try to reach a little farther back with your leg each time you practise this asana.

2. Raise your hands above your head with the fingers touching, and palms together. Very slowly bend your spine and your head backwards. When performed correctly this asana requires the outstretched leg, the spine and the arms to form a semicircle. Viewed from the side this Yoga posture looks like the flight of some graceful and powerful bird.

Please exercise very great care when bending your body backwards and do not try to force any of your muscles beyond their capacity. With practice they will loosen up and you will not experience any painful cramp in your shoulders and thighs. Beginners to Yoga, particularly those of you who are not used to taking exercise, may well find that your muscles are a little sore the day after you start. Do not exercise these muscles for a day or two but give them a rest as you try something different. So if, after attempting the WING POSTURE your shoulders are a little stiff the next day, then do some other exercise which involves another part of the body.

The study of Hatha Yoga in general will increase your natural patience so that, in time, you will be content to learn and improve slowly, and not expect dramatic results in next to no time. The study of Yoga requires infinite patience but in studying it you will gradually develop the patience you need. One cannot make this statement in connection with any other form of physical culture which proves once again that Hatha Yoga, though its province is primarily the physical body, is very much a mental discipline as well.

CHAPTER EIGHT

Asthma, bronchitis, and hay fever

INVARIABLY the first question I am asked about Yoga is, 'Do you stand on your head every morning?' To the uninitiated this standing on the head represents the sum total of Yoga, and it is thereupon dismissed as a foible of cranks and crackpots. Not one person in a hundred asks me *why* I stand on my head. In fact it does not cross the mind of the average person that it could possibly have any therapeutic value or indeed any value at all except to establish one as an eccentric. But if radiant good health is the lot of those who practise this Headstand, then 'long live eccentricity' say I.

But the Headstand or Sirshasana has not been called 'The King of Asanas' for nothing. You may wonder why I have waited until I reached more than half-way through this book before introducing you to this best known of all Yoga postures. Simply for the very good reason that it is difficult for the beginner to master and I wanted you to limber up with some easier exercises before attempting to balance on your head. I place the 'King of Asanas' in this chapter on disorders of the respiratory tract because in the relief and cure of such ailments as asthma, bronchitis, hay fever, nose troubles, and sinus troubles it has no equal.

Sinusitis, and allied complaints, often produce severe head-aches and acute discomfort in the cavities of the nose and face. It is difficult for doctors to reach these sinuses except by painful and unpleasant means and nasal sprays are of little use as the openings of the cavities are on the upper side and can only be drained when the body is inverted. This is where Yoga, and particularly the Headstand, is of great help.

So now let us try the preliminary stages.

The Headstand

1. Kneel down, sit back on your heels with your hands on your knees and then bend forward until your forehead touches the floor just in front of your knees. Remain in this position for a few moments and then slowly straighten up. The purpose of this simple exercise is to accustom the head to being lower than the body. If you experience any dizziness please straighten up immediately and proceed with extreme caution until you are able to remain with your head down without experiencing the slightest discomfort.

When you wish to go a stage further proceed as follows.

2. Kneel down as before, lace your fingers together and clasp your hands round the back of your head. Bend forward until your forehead touches the floor, approximately twelve inches away from your knees as in figure 24. Press the upper part of your body forward a few times, which will gradually accustom your head and neck to the unfamiliar pressure. Do not attempt the next stage until you can perform stage 2 without any discomfort.

3. In stage 3 you bring a little more of your weight on to your head and arms by straightening your legs with your heels off the ground as I have demonstrated in figure 25. Remain in this position for as long as you comfortably can and under no circumstances remain so if you are still experiencing any dizziness. Caution in the early stages of the Headstand will put you safely, and confidently, on your head.

4. After practising the first three stages carefully you are now ready to let your feet leave the ground. I always advise beginners to the Headstand to practise this, and the following stages, in a corner so that you have the support of the two walls. When you gain in confidence you can practise it against one wall and after that in the middle of the room. Meanwhile, let us return to stage 4. I advise you to put down a small pad or folded blanket for your head from now on. The pressure on the crown of your head is going to be considerable, especially in stages 5 and 6, and while Yoga asanas can sometimes be undeniably strenuous, even the most stoical of Gurus (Yoga Masters) would not wish

24   25

FIGURES 24, 25, 26, 27 HEADSTAND

26   27

to inflict any physical suffering on you. So I will wait while you bring that pad for your head.

Ready? Right, now kneel down in your corner with your hands laced behind your head. Adopt the position in figure 24. Raise yourself on to your toes but without straightening your legs. Walk on your toes for a couple of steps to bring your knees nearer to your face and then, with your knees bent give a little hop off the ground with both legs. You will find that your feet will leave the ground easily but they will also drop back equally easily. Be patient, you are more than half-way there. Make no attempt to go farther as this is the stage in the proceedings when students try to achieve too much in a hurry with sometimes unpleasant results. So perform this hopping off the ground three or four times and then straighten up for a rest.

There is an alternate way of performing stage 4 which some of you might find somewhat easier. Proceeding from the position in figure 24, rise on to your toes without straightening your legs and bring your knees nearer to your face as before. But this time, instead of trying to hop off the ground, very slowly press your body forwards until you can feel your toes leave the ground. Keep your body hunched up in a ball whichever method you adopt. If you do not you will be almost certain to overbalance at this stage. Practise stage 4 until you can make your toes leave the ground three times in succession. You will then, I hope, feel confident enough to proceed to stage 5.

5. This stage is an intensification of the last one. While I told you in stage 4 not to attempt anything beyond getting your toes to leave the ground for a brief instant, in this stage I would like you to increase the effort which you put into the whole movement until very gradually your body becomes less likely to drop back immediately. Proceed very slowly at this stage and remember at all times to keep your body rolled up into a ball with your knees well bent. Practise this stage frequently but do not prolong your efforts to the point when you begin to tire. It is far better to practise stage 5 only half a dozen times at once. You can go back to it later when you have had a short rest.

Stage 5 may be frustrating in the extreme to you when you are impatient to rise into the Headstand but I assure you that if you have been practising the preliminary stages properly, in a shorter time than you imagine you will find that your body does not drop back to the ground as you expected, but remains poised at the half-way mark. Your knees will sail up right past your head and you will find, if you keep perfectly still (and don't jerk about in sheer surprise), that you will be able to remain so for a few seconds. Now you are really getting somewhere. But again I must ask you to be patient and not, please not, to try and straighten your legs. Be content, just for a little while longer, to keep your knees bent and your body rolled up into a ball and to aim for this all-important and controlling half-way position. You will not find it particularly comfortable but you will feel safe and confident if you practise in a corner so that there is no danger whatever of you overbalancing or falling. The pad under your head will add greatly to your comfort.

6. When you are able to remain immobile at the half-way point for a second or two, proceed as follows. When you either take your jump off the ground or press your body forward to make your feet leave the ground do so with more force than you have hitherto been using so that instead of stopping at the half-way point you will swing your legs right over and with your knees still bent your feet will touch the wall as I have demonstrated in figure 26. You will find this stage very easy if you have been practising properly, and you will be able to remain in this position for a full minute or more without the slightest effort or discomfort. Come down, please, as soon as you feel the slightest strain on your head, neck, or shoulders.

7. In this last and final stage of the Headstand you have three alternatives, according to your individual capabilities. I will describe first what is generally considered to be the easiest method. While balanced as in figure 26, very gradually tuck in your buttocks, bring your feet away from the wall, and at the same time very slowly straighten your legs. Your feet will swing right back to the wall at first but do practise straightening your legs even if at first you cannot manage without resting your feet against the wall. Having got so far with the Headstand you will

find that this final stage is the slowest of all. I know it is frustrating, but once you can do the Headstand you will have it for life, so it is worth a little of your time and patience now, is it not?

The second method is as follows. Proceed from the position in figure 26, but this time straighten your legs while keeping your feet against the wall. You will be in a kind of Headstand at once by this method but why I do not favour it as much as the other one is that in this position your spine is uncomfortably arched instead of being held naturally and because it shows quick results students tend to rely on this method and become so used to the support of the wall that they have difficulty, afterwards, in doing the Headstand without it. So really this second method takes more time in the long run.

The third method is as follows. Proceed from the hunched up half-way position and, instead of swinging your feet over to touch the wall, very slowly, half-inch by half-inch straighten your legs. You will wobble, you will fall all over the place, you will drop back to the ground like a stone and you will probably become convinced that you will never make it at all, but again take heart and keep practising. Patience is the only way and one day you will find that, instead of bouncing back to the floor as you expected, you will remain poised on your head and arms with your body as straight as a candle, as in figure 27, page 83.

I must warn you that, like so many others, when you first find that you can do the Headstand, you will be so surprised that you will probably overbalance and have to come down quickly out of sheer amazement. It is rather like learning to ride a bicycle. When you finally find yourself gaily pedalling along without someone propping you up, you look around, find you have left your friend far behind and promptly fall off in sheer horror. So while you are still flushed with your first success, try your Headstand again. This time you will find that you can control your muscles to such an extent that you will be able to rise slowly into a beautiful Headstand. There you are. You finally made it. Congratulations!

Remember that when you are practising do keep your body rolled up into a ball with your knees near your face both going up and coming down. When you can do a perfect Headstand it will be of more benefit to you to perform it several times a day for short periods, say five or ten minutes at a time, rather than to indulge in long spells of half an hour or more. There is sóme controversy on this point but I favour the 'little and often' method as being not only more beneficial but also more practical for the business person or busy housewife. Hatha Yoga is nothing if not down to earth and practical.

The variations of the Headstand are many and the adventurous among my readers might like to try a few, though please apply the same care in each case when coming down. Roll your body into a ball and so avoid spills.

Variation 1. Your hands, instead of being laced behind your head, are kept separate. As you rise into the Headstand the hands should be flat on the floor, palms downwards, about six inches on either side of your head. While in this position you may either straighten your legs as already described or bend your knees and place the soles of your feet together. This stretches the muscles of the shoulders and thighs.

Variation 2. In the above position the legs are crossed at the knees and again at the ankles. This tones and stretches the muscles of the thighs and legs and helps to relieve varicose veins.

Variation 3. Again in the above position with the hands on either side of the head, stretch your legs as wide apart as possible until you are doing the splits upside down.

Variation 4. Here the hands are in a different position. Before you rise into the Headstand, raise your arms above your head with the elbows bent, with your hands grasping the opposite forearms. Now rise into position and keep your legs straight up in the air.

Variation 5. Perform the classical Headstand with the hands laced at the back of the head and then, with your feet together, bring your legs forward until they are at right angles to your body.

Variation 6. This is one of the most advanced Yoga asanas called Oorhwapadmasana or the HEADSTAND LOTUS POSE. While in the Headstand fold your legs into the Lotus Pose and remain thus for as long as you can. This one is not for the beginner but the practised student will find it surprisingly easy.

Variation 7. If you can perform the Headstand Lotus Position you can proceed a step farther. While in this position twist the body from the waist to the right, to the left, and so on from side to side. This exercises the muscles of the waistline and sheers off fat in this area.

Variation 8. Still in the Headstand Lotus Pose bring your crossed legs down until your body is bent double. This needs especial care when you are coming out of it. Do so as follows. Straighten your body first, uncross your legs, stretch them up in the air, bend your knees, and descend with safety.

Variation 9. Though I could take up a whole chapter on describing the many variations of the Headstand I will make this the last one because I would like you to go on to something else which many of you will find a little easier. In this variation of the Headstand the first and last variations are combined. Here the hands are placed on either side of the head, the legs are then crossed in the Lotus Position and the legs are brought down until the body is bent double. Again please take care when coming out of the position.

Benefits of the Headstand

This asana affects four of the most important endocrine glands —the pituitary, the pineal, the thyroid, and the parathyroids. The regular practice of the Headstand helps to relieve insomnia, tension, nervousness and anxiety, poor circulation of the blood, asthma, bronchitis, sinusitis, hay fever, headaches, female disorders, and lack of energy. It is because of its many benefits and because it affects the most important gland in the body, the pituitary, that the Headstand has been called 'The King of Asanas'.

A word of warning, though. If you suffer from high blood pressure, palpitations, chronic constipation, chronic nasal catarrh, or weak eyes, please *do not attempt* the Headstand. Cure your complaints by other Yoga exercises first, but in the case of high blood pressure I do not recommend it under any circumstances.

Having just described, in this chapter on disorders of the respiratory tract, one of the most difficult of the Yoga asanas, I will now describe a really easy one which will present not the slightest difficulty. It is an invaluable exercise for sufferers from these complaints because it allows full expansion of the lungs while doing deep breathing and at the same time the inverted position helps to drain congested cavities. It is called THE LETTER L BREATHING EXERCISE.

Letter L Breathing Exercise

Facing a convenient wall, lie down on your back and place your feet as high up the wall as you possibly can, keeping your legs straight. Stretch out your arms above your head, without joining the fingers, and hold them palms upwards and elbows straight. Your body is now in the shape of a letter L as in figure 28, page 91.

Perform the deep slow Complete Breath while in this position. Take as many breaths as you have time for, but not less than ten at a time. Do not use force and at the end of each exhalation pull in your abdomen slightly to expel the last small amount of air from your lungs. This exercise will not only help to bring relief from asthma, bronchitis, sinusitis, and hay fever, but the inverted posture will bring calmness to your mind.

Having had an easy time of it with the Letter L Breathing Exercise, try now another exercise which incorporates breathing, stretching, and in its advanced stages, a high degree of balance. It is the beautiful MOUNTAIN POSTURE or PARVATASANA in Sanskrit.

Mountain Posture

There are four variations of this posture and I will describe them in order of difficulty.

Variation 1. Kneel down and hold your body straight up from the knees to the top of your head. Raise your arms above your head and hold them palm to palm while keeping your elbows as straight as you can. Practise the Yoga Complete Breath while in this position and remember not to let your body sag and to keep your tummy muscles pulled well in.

Variation 2. Sit down in the Lotus Pose, raise your hands above your head with your fingertips touching as in figure 31. Holding your body very still, and without letting your arms sag, again practise the Yoga Complete Breath. Keep this up for as long as you can but if you feel any discomfort in your legs please undo them.

Variation 3. This increases the stretch of the dorsal muscles while you are performing the deep breathing. While seated in the Lotus Pose lace your fingers together and turn them palms upwards. Now raise your arms as far above your head as you can and you will feel a powerful stretch along your sides. This intensifies the benefits of this asana. I have demonstrated the correct position in figure 30, page 91.

Variation 4. This is one of the most spectacular of the Yoga asanas and is for more advanced students. Although this is primarily a book for beginners to the subject I did not want to leave out this fourth variation of the Mountain Posture in case some of you might feel up to trying it. It is not easy but the practice of it will help you to acquire balance and patience. While sitting in the Lotus Pose with your hands above your head with the fingertips touching as in figure 31, raise your buttocks off the floor and remain balanced on your knee-caps as I have demonstrated in figure 29.

To the adventurous among you who attempt it I would say please go carefully and do not strain any of your muscles. You will achieve nothing by forcing your unwilling muscles where they would rather not go. Your best way to master Variation 4 is to practise the other three until perfect and then, while supporting yourself with a conveniently placed chair or low table you can gently pull yourself on to your knee-caps, and then let go of the chair or table. It will tax your sense of balance to the utmost but practice will be the answer. While poised on your knee-caps with your arms above your head practise the Yoga Complete Breath. The effort needed for the perfection of this

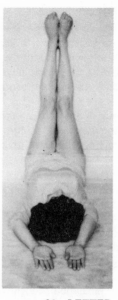

FIGURE 28 LETTER "L" EXERCISE

FIGURE 29 ADVANCED MOUNTAIN POSTURE

FIGURES 30, 31 MOUNTAIN POSTURE

advanced posture will greatly improve your powers of concentration and in addition to the benefits to the muscles of the arms and torso the deep breathing will help congested lungs and bronchial tubes and the posture tones up the entire nervous system.

In a chapter devoted to complaints of the respiratory tract one would expect that most of the exercises would be breathing ones and so they are. Here is one which is called THE BELLOWS BREATH, or BHASTRIKA.

However deeply we inhale and however thoroughly we exhale, there always remains in the lungs a residue of stale air. It is vital to clear this out to ensure a complete renovation of air and Yoga's unique method of doing this is this exercise.

1. Sit down on a hard chair with your feet flat on the floor, your hands on your knees palms down and your spine erect. Do not let your tummy muscles sag. While sitting up straight, slowly and deeply inhale.

2. When you have completed your inhalation suddenly bend forward from the waist until your head touches your knees or as near to them as you can get and at the same time exhale with as much force as you can. This is one of the few times in Yoga that you *should* use force.

The bending forward movement will squeeze every bit of stale air from your lungs.

3. As you slowly straighten up begin inhaling again and complete your inhalation while sitting up straight. Then exhale with force once more and at the same time bend your body forward until your head touches your knees.

Perform the BELLOWS BREATH only twice at first but gradually increase the number of breaths you take until you are doing it twelve times a day. Add one extra breath per week. After every fourth inhalation retain the breath for up to six seconds and then exhale immediately while bending forward once more. Do not perform the Bellows Breath to excess. Twelve times is enough even for the advanced student.

The benefits of this exercise, apart from cleansing the lungs and bronchial passages, are the toning up of the whole lung action with highly stimulating effects on the entire body. The bending forward and straightening movements help to relieve constipation, and as you know by now, anything that is an enemy of constipation is a friend of the body. So this exercise is as useful as it is simple to perform.

And now for something more difficult but equally beneficial. This is another asana with an animal name, called MATSY-ASANA or the FISH POSTURE. In this exercise the chest is allowed to expand fully during deep breathing, and it also removes stiffness of the neck and shoulders and so is a useful exercise with which to follow the Shoulderstand described in chapter four. It also strengthens the thyroid and parathyroid glands and tones up the circulation of the blood. If you suffer from excessive cold in the winter this is a good exercise to warm yourself. There are three variations of THE FISH POSTURE and I will start with the easiest for all beginners.

Variation 1. Lie flat on your back with your legs outstretched and feet together. With the help of your elbows raise your chest and bend your head as far back as you can until the crown is touching the floor. Try to hold this position for thirty seconds, and then very slowly lower your body to the floor. Relax for a few moments before proceeding to:

Variation 2. A little more difficult, this one. Sit down in the Lotus Pose, and with the help of your elbows bend your body backwards very slowly. Bend your head back as far as you possibly can until the crown is resting on the floor. Grasp your toes with your fingers and arch your spine as fully as you possibly can. Remain thus for up to thirty seconds and then relax. (See Fig. 32, page 95.)

Variation 3. Proceed as above but instead of grasping your toes with your fingers place your hands behind your head with your arms crossed or else with your fingers laced together and placed just behind your neck.

If you are still having difficulty with the Lotus Pose, and I know that many of you will take quite some time to master it as it is very difficult for the average Westerner, then perform the easiest of the variations of this posture until you can go a stage farther. In all three of the variations practise the Yoga Complete Breath and it is a good place here to remind you that this Complete Breath should be performed slowly and fully. There should be no rushing over it. It is far better to take two or three really deep breaths than half a dozen shallow ones. All you hurried business people take note! The Yoga Complete Breath while performed when the body is in the Fish Posture helps to remove the spasm from the bronchial tubes and also helps to relieve asthma.

As with many of the Yoga asanas, this posture has a variation for advanced students only. I include it here for the sake of interest and in case there may be some readers adventurous enough to attempt it.

Variation 4. Begin in the Lotus Pose once more but this time instead of levering yourself backwards on your elbows bend forward very slowly until your face is touching the floor. You will feel considerable pressure on your hip joints so please be careful not to strain yourself. Remain thus for a few seconds only and then straighten up immediately. When you can perform this variation with ease, and it can be done easily with patient practice, gradually extend the period when your face is touching the floor, and then try to practice the Yoga Complete Breath. After this variation lie flat on your back and relax for a few minutes.

I will end this chapter with the joker of the pack so far as Yoga is concerned. Although a highly effective and useful exercise, it entails pulling a grotesque face, however, as Yoga is best done in solitude there should not be anyone around to take fright! Hatha Yoga being a complete science no part of the body has been overlooked, including the throat and tongue, and there is a unique exercise for this area known as SIMHASANA, the LION POSTURE.

Method. Kneel down on the floor, hands on your knees palms upwards, and then sit back on your heels. Very slowly inhale, and when you have completed your inhalation hold your breath for an instant and then exhale through the mouth with as much force as you can. At the end of your exhalation stick out your

FIGURE 32 FISH POSTURE

tongue as far as you possibly can to the point of gagging. At the same time tense every muscle in your body including your arms and fingers, pop your eyes and generally make yourself look like a gargoyle. The more gruesome the face the more benefit you will derive from this exercise. Retain this unaesthetic posture for as long as you comfortably can without inhaling and then relax and breathe naturally for a few seconds. Then repeat the LION POSTURE up to six times in every practice session and particularly if you suffer from any form of chronic condition of the throat or tongue. You will find that the practice of Simhasana will relieve a sore throat more quickly than the most powerful drugs or lozenges, as it supplies the throat and tongue with a richer supply of blood which is nature's own cure. The LION POSTURE is beloved of singers and actors whose voices are part of their livelihood and I recommend it to anyone who has any public speaking to do.

Ideally all Yoga asanas should be performed in the open air in order to draw into the lungs the maximum amount of fresh air. However, not everyone is lucky enough to have a garden in which case you should always practise before an open window. In the case of exercises for asthma, bronchitis, and allied complaints mentioned in this chapter, this is a vital necessity.

CHAPTER NINE

Arthritis and rheumatism

ONE of Yoga's answers to the problems with which this chapter is concerned reads a little like black magic. Still it adds a touch of the bizarre and the exotic to this exacting science of discipline and, as with all Yoga practices, there is sound good sense behind its methods. The Indians claim that people who are afflicted with arthritis or allied complaints should keep a raw, unpeeled, winter-crop potato—yes, I did say a potato!—close to their skin day and night until the condition is relieved. It sounds a little like an old gipsy legend and as a matter of fact I did meet a gipsy some time ago who was afflicted with arthritis in the shoulders. I told him this Yoga story about keeping a potato near one's skin and he looked at me in sheer amazement. He was completely puzzled as to how I had got hold of this old 'gipsy' secret, so it seems that way back in time, gipsy or Yogi, they had respect for the humble potato as a powerful cure for arthritis.

It need not be a very large potato as apparently the smaller ones work just as efficiently and I must say more conveniently. An over-large potato carried upon the person could lead to all kinds of questions and complications. The potato should be discarded when it either grows very hard like a stone or else becomes soft and wrinkled, and should be replaced by a fresh one, but make quite sure it is a winter-crop one.

You could keep it in your pocket during the day and at night slip it into the toe of an old stocking and draw the other end over your hand so that the potato does not roll away from you while you sleep. If you are married this practice could produce some hilarity from your partner but the laugh would be yours if you cured your arthritis by this unorthodox method.

So bear with the jeers of your mate and try the experiment. You may be agreeably surprised.

For good measure, while you are on the potato cure, you should drink potato water, which is one of the very best alkalizing drinks and helps the system to eliminate the impurities which are to blame for your complaint. To prepare this drink, and it need not be unpalatable if you flavour it well, wash four or five fairly large potatoes but do not peel them. Put them in a saucepan with two pints of water and bring to the boil. Simmer them slowly for about an hour and then strain through a fine sieve or cloth. Drink the water first thing in the morning, at least once or twice during the day, and just before you slip your hand into that stocking with the potato in it before you hop into bed at night. If you visit your local health shop you will find all kinds of vegetable extracts and salts with which to make your potato water more drinkable.

It is also highly beneficial to arthritis sufferers to eat one or two finely grated raw potatoes, including the skin, every day. I know it sounds revolting but, added to soups, stews, salads or vegetables just before serving you would hardly know it was there! However, your system will know it is there and react in a very favourable way. It is worth trying is it not? and I would be most interested to hear from my readers who notice an improvement in their condition through the 'potato cure'.

But let us now turn this from a cookery book back into a book on Hatha Yoga! Here is an exercise known as HALASANA or the PLOUGH POSTURE. One of the basic Yoga asanas, it stretches the vertebrae to the maximum, and subjects the abdomen and its organs and muscles to a powerful massage. The nerve centre and cells along the spine are stimulated as they receive a richer supply of blood. By practising this exercise your spine will gradually become more elastic and as it effects the kidneys it is a powerful way of eliminating the toxic waste that is the primary cause of arthritis and allied complaints. Waste is the foundation of all disease. It cannot flourish if the body is purified. And now for the PLOUGH POSTURE. (See page 137.)

1. Lie down on your back, feet together and hands along your sides. Raise your legs and buttocks off the ground and as you put your hands on your hips to steady yourself push your legs

over your head while keeping your knees straight. The first stage of the Plough Posture is pictured in figure 44, page 137.

2. Bend your legs backwards until your toes touch the ground. Press your chin firmly against your chest in a chin lock and place your hands, palms down, facing the opposite way to your legs. Your body now roughly resembles an old-fashioned plough. Try to increase the stretch of your spine by pushing your toes away from your head as far as you can. I have demonstrated the correct position in figure 45. Your hands may be placed in two other ways if you wish. One way is to lace them together and . place them behind your head just above the neck and the other is to keep them on the hips as in stage one. Indeed this way may help you to push your body over a little more and increase the stretch of the spine.

Some of my older readers may find difficulty with Halasana at first so try it this way. Take your starting position with your head two, three, or more feet away from the wall according to your height and convenience. When you swing your legs over your head your toes will touch the wall. Try then to walk down the wall with your toes, but gently please. Do not try to force your toes lower down the wall than they will comfortably go, otherwise an enraged and rigid muscle could repay your lack of consideration by giving you agony for weeks, which would have the effect of scaring you away for evermore from this most valuable posture. So careful, please.

When you are able to perform this Plough Posture to your liking try to increase, all the time, the overall stretch, as this position is most beneficial when carried to its extreme form, i.e. with the toes at the maximum distance from the head and the chin pressed firmly into the middle of the chest, as in the illustration.

The way you unwind yourself from the Plough Posture is equally important as the way you get into it. Performed in its correct way, the unwinding of the Plough requires considerable muscular control so, as always, go slowly at first and constant practice will give you the control you need. As you unwind this posture keep your head on the floor throughout until you return to the starting position flat on your back. Your natural tendency will be to raise your head as you unwind but, although you must do it this way when you first begin, always bear in mind what you are aiming for. The keeping of your head on the floor increases the work on your dorsal and abdominal muscles and gives them a very powerful massage and exercise. As you unwind bend your knees as this will make things easier for you than keeping them straight, and above all unwind *slowly*. This posture is, as you will have realized by now, deceptively simple looking. Graceful in execution and beautiful in its static stage, nevertheless it uses a lot of muscles which you may seldom have used before in this particular manner, and it also requires a high degree of muscular control to perform it to perfection.

When you can do this classical Plough Posture perfectly you might like to try three variations, just to add variety to your daily practice schedule. In each case the posture will limber the spine, keep it more supple and youthful and therefore discourage arthritis and rheumatism.

Variation 1. This differs from the Halasana I have just described only in the position of the arms. This time they should be outstretched and pointing the same way as your legs so that you can touch your toes with your fingers.

Variation 2. Execute the first Plough Posture I described and then move the legs as far apart as possible, remaining thus for as long as you comfortably can. This imparts an extra stretch to the muscles of the legs and thighs.

Variation 3. This variation of the Plough Posture is called Karna Peedasana or the *Ear to Knee Posture*.

Proceeding from the Plough Posture, draw your knees up to your ears, your legs remaining flat on the ground from your knees to your toes. Bend your arms and place your hands behind your knees in order to keep them pressed to the floor. Only the most supple among my readers will be able to do this at first but regular practice of the other variations will limber your spine sufficiently for the Ear to Knee Posture.

Whichever variation of the Plough Posture you perform, do not omit the Yoga Complete Breath while remaining in this static pose. Your chest will be somewhat restricted and you may possibly find that the taking of a deep breath is a little uncomfortable at first, but do keep trying and you will find it gets easier as you practice. No Yoga asana should be performed unless it is in conjunction with Yoga breathing. The one complements the other to affect the entire organism.

The following exercise will help those who suffer from calcium deposits at the shoulder joints. Sit down in the Lotus Posture, or if you cannot yet do this sit down in the Easy Pose. If this too is beyond you sit down on a hard chair with your back straight. Raise your right hand and bring it behind your shoulder and at the same time bend your left hand behind your back and join your two hands together. I mentioned this position of the hands earlier in connection with the Bull Posture for sciatica but sufferers from arthritis and rheumatism in the shoulders will also greatly benefit from this simple arm exercise. Remain in the position for as long as you comfortably can and then perform it with reversed arms. Practise this exercise at any time of the day you possibly can and incidentally, if you have round shoulders it will greatly improve this condition.

I will end this chapter with another breathing exercise which most of you will find easy and pleasant to perform. It is called the WINDMILL breathing exercise and again will help to rid the body of calcium deposits and tone the nerves and muscles of the back, shoulders, and arms.

1. Standing legs apart inhale very slowly and deeply through the mouth. At the same time lift your arms sideways to shoulder height, palms downward. Complete your inhalation.

2. While holding the breath swing the arms, upwards and backwards three times in succession like a windmill, and then in the opposite direction three times. This should be done rhythmically and without hurry.

3. Exhale with some force through the mouth as you slowly lower your arms. Finish this exercise standing up straight and performing a few Yoga Complete Breaths.

If you suffer from arthritis or rheumatism practise the exercises in this chapter faithfully and don't forget that potato will you!

CHAPTER TEN

Obesity and the improvement of the figure

THIS chapter, I have no doubt, is the one to which the majority of women will turn first. Knowing as you do that Yoga can give you a perfect figure you have made this your main reason for pursuing the subject. I assure you this is no worse a reason for beginning the study of Yoga than any other. There cannot really be a bad reason for wanting to do something good, and though Yoga offers much in the way of a peaceful and healthy existence your main concern, at this stage anyway, is how to get that pad of fat off your hips and reduce that bulging tummy. So be it. I will show you the way and as you learn more and more of Yoga perhaps eventually your reason for studying it will be a more spiritual one.

There is little need to explain to you the connection between obesity and your health. Apart from being aesthetically all wrong it puts a strain on the heart, the internal organs, the legs and feet and in fact the entire body. It is dangerous to be overweight. It is your duty to improve your figure for the sake of your health, your peace of mind and your general well being.

But before I explain how Yoga can help you to regain a slim, supple, and graceful figure I must impress on you right at the beginning that there is no magic formula which will sheer those extra pounds off you while you go on eating four square meals a day with snacks in between and goodness knows how many cups of tea sweetened with sugar. In short, Yoga is not black magic. It is sheer common sense. It will help you if you are prepared to help yourself.

In presenting various Yoga asanas in this chapter I must again impress on you that these alone will not make you lose weight. Yoga you see is a *way of life* not just a system of physical culture.

102

FIGURE 33   ANGLE BALANCE

You must study Yoga as a *whole* and let it pervade every part of your life. Let it gradually alter your way of thinking and in time it will affect your attitude towards food. For many people food is a social occasion, or a means of chopping up the day. To very many others it is a form of sheer solid comfort in times of stress or anxiety. To still others it is a hobby or a release from boredom. They don't know what to do with themselves so they eat—and grow fat.

I do not suggest that you try drastically to alter your eating habits as soon as you read this book. Let Yoga gently do that for you. Practise Yoga as a complete science, and very slowly adjust your eating habits according to your state of mind. By this I mean that at the moment, maybe food is of major importance to you. It is right that you have this incentive to eat for it is necessary to take food in order to live, but many people, far *too* many, take far more food than they need. This results in a gradual build up of fat in the body until there you are—two, three, or even more stones overweight. It is never easy to take off weight and Yoga is not a short cut by any means, but this much I promise you. That once you have slimmed, the Yoga way, you will be able to eat as you please and not gain an ounce. Yoga, in affecting the glands, establishes a rhythm in the body so that you do not feel a desire for food that you do not *need*. You want to eat only enough to keep superbly fit. Your new calmness of mind will make it unnecessary for you to turn to food for comfort or as a means of relieving tension or boredom. As I have said, Yoga will affect your way of life, even against your will; it will alter your attitude towards many things and one of these things is the food you eat.

Having warned you that I have no magic formula dreamed up by the ancient Yogis with regard to recovering a slim, beautiful figure, let me discuss the first step in this 'battle of the bulge'. The majority of overweight people suffer from chronic constipation, so one of your very first tasks is to turn back to chapter five, re-read all I have written, and vow to make an immediate onslaught on your sluggish bowels, as this complaint is very fattening as well as uncomfortable. Practise all the Yoga asanas described in the chapter on constipation, and in particular practise the water-drinking habits of the Yogis and the relaxing and contracting movements known as *Uddiyani*. This ridding your body of excessive waste, and the practice of Yoga asanas and breathing exercises will go a long way towards sheering that superfluous fat from your body and here is a Yoga asana which will help you on your way. It is called the SIDESLIP and it should not present too much difficulty if you spend the first couple of days limbering up your torso with the following simple movements.

Limbering up Exercises

1. Stand up straight, feet together, arms raised to shoulder level.

2. Holding your arms steady swing them as far as possible round to the right.

Twist your body to the maximum to bring your right arm as far round as you can and at the same time turn your head to look over your right shoulder so that you twist your neck to the utmost; as you turn slowly bend your left arm so that when the swing to the right is at its height your left thumb should touch your right shoulder.

3. Hold this position for a few seconds and then repeat the swing to the other side. You can repeat these swings *ad lib* but at first it is as well to limit yourself to a maximum of six if you have never taken any exercise before.

Two points to remember. These swinging movements from side to side should be performed slowly and rhythmically. Emphasis is on the full sweep of the arms and the twisting of your torso to the utmost rather than on speed. Speed isn't a word used in Yoga, rather substitute the word pressure. At the extreme points of the twisting movement you can exert a slight pressure to enhance the value of this limbering exercise. And having practised it for a day or two you should graduate with no difficulty to a more advanced lateral twist called THE SIDE-SLIP POSTURE.

1. Kneel down on the floor and sit back on your heels. Raise

your arms above your head, clasp your hands together and turn them palms upwards.

2. Slide your body off your heels to the right and at the same time gently swing your arms towards the opposite side. I have demonstrated the correct movement in figure 34. You should not bend forward while performing this movement but move from the waist to the side only.

3. Now raise your body off the floor, swing it slowly and gently to the other side and at the same time swing your arms over to the opposite side. Try to keep your knees *together* throughout the Sideslip Posture, but if you find this difficult or impossible at first you may hold your knees apart to maintain your balance but at all times endeavour to bring your knees together.

Many people, while attempting this asana for the first time have difficulty with stage 3, that is the lifting of the body off the floor and the swinging it to the other side. In fact some people have trouble in getting themselves off the floor at all in this position and others, if they do succeed, land with a great thump on the opposite side and have difficulty getting up from there. Be patient. This exercise is not quite so easy as it looks. Graceful, and a great favourite with women everywhere, it looks simple enough but in actual fact it requires a high degree of muscular control and concentration.

Remember your head while you are doing the SIDESLIP POSTURE. It should bend the same way as your arms, which you should, throughout the movement, try to press backwards as far as possible to avoid any possible sagging forward of your body.

This asana is one of the finest in the entire Yoga range for slimming the waist and reducing that pad of fat which often settles on top of the hipbones. You will feel a powerful stretch from your hips to your armpits and if you do this exercise correctly you will feel rather sore in the region of your hip joints the next day. This is normal and it will prove to you that this Yoga exercise has already begun to work for you. While one side of your body is being stretched the other side is being

107

FIGURE 34 SIDESLIP

FIGURE 35 STANDING BEND

powerfully contracted. You can feel it squeezing the fatty tissue. It also imparts a healthy massage to the organs and muscles of the abdomen and helps the torso towards a new suppleness and grace.

When you can perform the SIDESLIP POSTURE at a moderate speed and with some degree of muscular control, then try to slow down the whole process so that it becomes a study in slow and gentle motion. This calls for a much higher degree of muscular control and thus the benefits of the posture are greatly enhanced. When you have perfected your movements in slow motion regulate your deep breathing so that you lean to one side while inhaling and to the other while exhaling. Rhythm and slow motion are the final keywords in this exercise.

In its perfect form the Sideslip Posture should be as follows. Lean to the right while inhaling. Remain immobile as you complete your inhalation and hold your breath for as long as possible. When the impulse to exhale appears do so as you raise your body off the floor and swing it to the other side. Remain immobile as you complete your exhalation and remain holding your breath for as long as possible before inhaling again. This constitutes one round. Perform up to a dozen rounds a day, starting with four and adding two rounds per week.

Like the Sideslip Posture this next exercise is not so easy as it looks. It is called AROHANASANA or in English THE RAISED HEAD AND LEGS POSTURE. This asana wages war on that bulging abdomen.

1. Lie flat on your back with your legs outstretched and your feet together. Lace your fingers together and place them at the back of your head just above your neck.

2. Inhale very slowly and deeply and at the same time raise your head, shoulders, and legs off the floor remembering to keep your knees straight. Hold this position until you have completed your inhalation. I have demonstrated the correct position in figure 36, page 111.

3. After holding your breath for a few seconds very slowly return to the original position.

These instructions are simplicity itself and even the photograph of me lying with my head, shoulders and legs raised can give you little idea of the sheer muscular effort involved in holding them that way. But try it for yourself. Those two words 'very slowly', in connection with the lowering of the legs will catch most of you out at first. You will want to plop your legs down on the floor in a great rush, but try as hard as you can to resist this impulse. It is the easy way out and you will gain nothing from employing it. You want to reduce that abdomen don't you? Then do please remember that there is no hurry at all in this exercise, and the slow s-l-o-w lowering of the legs is precisely what strengthens, tones, exercises, and reduces those flabby abdominal muscles and helps to reduce fat in this area.

This is an exercise that requires a lot of patient practice before you can perform it perfectly. As it is a strenuous posture do not do it more than twice a day for the first few days and after that very gradually increase the number of times you do it up to six.

In addition to toning and strengthening the abdominal muscles and reducing excess fat this exercise also helps to relieve constipation so it is doubly beneficial to the would-be-slimmer. The back and shoulders are also strengthened by the slow motion lifting and lowering of the head and shoulders.

A word of warning. This is *not* an exercise for women during pregnancy or who have any internal disorders, and people with hernia should practise it with extreme caution.

For those readers who find the Arohanasana too strenuous or simply beyond you, here is a similar though much easier exercise which is called UDHITTA PADASANA or THE RAISED LEG POSTURE.

1. Lie on your back with your legs outstretched and feet together. Inhale slowly and deeply and at the same time raise your right leg, keeping the knee straight, until it is at right angles to your body as in figure 37, page 111.

2. Remain thus as you complete your inhalation, hold your breath for a few seconds while keeping absolutely still, your other leg flat on the floor.

3. When the impulse to exhale appears do so and at the same time very slowly lower your leg. Repeat with the other leg.

This simple exercise may be performed once or twice a day until you feel you are ready to try it with both legs at once. This exercise, like the previous one will help to break up fatty tissue in the abdominal area. I must warn beginners to this, and the previous exercise that they might find their abdominal muscles a little sore the day after starting as you are using muscles which may never have been used in that way before. Do not worry about the discomfort. It means that Yoga is working for you so you should welcome it as a sign that you were performing the exercise properly. Remember always to lower your legs s-l-o-w-l-y.

Let us now try a standing posture for the improvement of the figure. This one will keep your spine healthy and supple, reduce abdominal fat, tone up sluggish bowels, and slim your waist. It is called THE WOODCUTTER Exercise.

1. Stand erect, feet far apart. Stretch out your arms, lace your fingers together and imagine that you are holding a very heavy axe.

2. Inhale slowly and deeply and at the same time slowly raise the 'axe' above your head until you are leaning back as far as you can without losing your balance. I have demonstrated this backward bending position in figure 40, page 112.

3. Remain in the backward bend as you complete your inhalation, remain immobile for a few seconds holding your breath.

4. When the impulse to exhale appears swing the 'axe' down slowly as though there were actually a log in front of you and you were chopping it up. The downward movement should be a very powerful one but do not stop when you reach the imaginary log but let your hands follow through your legs as in figure 39.

Repeat this exercise six times, and do watch the following four points. Firstly that your elbows should be straight throughout, secondly that your feet should be firmly planted on the floor without moving, thirdly that you do not move your buttocks whilst you are bending down, and lastly that all the movement should be done from *above* the waist. The lower half of the body should remain absolutely still.

FIGURE 36   RAISED HEAD AND LEGS POSE

FIGURE 37   RAISED LEG   FIGURE 38   TRIANGLE BEND

39   FIGURES 39, 40 WOODCHOPPER 40

41   FIGURES 41, 42 TRIANGLE 42

A word of warning. This is a rather strenuous exercise and I do not recommend it for women with internal complaints or people with weak hearts. This exercise should not be done during menstruation.

The next posture for reducing abdominal fat is called THE TRIANGLE BEND.

1. Stand erect with your hands clasped together behind your back. Your feet should be far apart with your knees straight.

2. Inhale slowly and at the same time turn your torso, from the waist upwards, slightly to the right. Continue with your inhalation as you bend your head slowly until your forehead touches your right knee. Your hands should still be clasped behind your back. I have demonstrated the position in figure 38.

3. Remain in this position for as long as you comfortably can without exhaling, and when the impulse to exhale appears do so, at the same time slowly straightening up.

4. Repeat the movement to the other side, bending your head towards the left knee.

That is the Triangle Bend. Repeat it twice each way at first but when you are limbered up you can perform it up to half a dozen times. Did I hear some of you say 'impossible'. I'll admit that if you are very stiff, or very much overweight, the Triangle Bend may well seem so, but again I must ask you to practise it, without straining, and you will soon be pleasantly surprised at how easy this exercise really is. It reduces fat on the abdomen, waist, and thighs.

And now for another posture which has a similar name. This is TRIKONASANA or THE TRIANGLE POSTURE, and you may find it easier than the previous one. It is one of the most effective Yoga asanas for reducing fat round the waistline, the hips, the upper arms, and the thighs, and it should present little difficulty even to the beginner.

Trikonasana

1. Stand erect, feet far apart, and your arms extended sideways at shoulder level. This is the starting position as in figure 41.

2. While keeping your head in the same position (that is not

turning it) bend slowly to the right until your right hand touches your right foot. You will have to bend your right knee a little to do this and at the same time your left leg should remain out-stretched to maintain balance.

3. Your left arm should be gradually brought up and over your head as far as possible, as I have demonstrated in figure 42.

4. Remain in this position until you have completed your inhalation.

5. When the impulse to inhale appears do so and at the same time slowly return to the starting position. Repeat this exercise to the other side.

The most important feature of this exercise is the gradual increase of the stretch of the free arm, which should be brought over farther and farther each time you practise this exercise. It should be performed four times a day at first and when you become more flexible it can be performed up to a dozen times a day. The accent is on slow and rhythmical movement, as this exercise is much more beneficial to the health and the figure when performed slowly and gracefully. The breathing should also be carefully timed to coincide with the appropriate movements. Trikonasana is not a very strenuous posture but all the same I do not advise it for women with any kind of internal disorders or for people suffering from hernia.

This being the last of the so-called 'slimming' Yoga asanas, I should like to lend a helping hand to those of you who, with the best will in the world to practise Yoga and grow slim, feel that you cannot find the time to practise. I know it isn't always easy especially if you go out to business as the mornings are filled with rushing about, and breakfasts and bath water, and if something has to be left out—well that's Yoga isn't it? This is one of the main reasons, I find, why would-be devotees of Yoga do not pursue the subject.

In view of the fact that Yoga asanas should be done on an empty stomach it is usually convenient to perform your practice schedule first thing in the morning when you get out of bed. You may feel you are too sleepy to do them then but you will find that some of the asanas are very bracing owing to their stimulating effect on the nervous system and soon give you a wide-awake feeling. And once you have established the habit of doing Yoga postures first thing in the morning it should become as much a part of your routine as having your morning bath or cleaning your teeth. So, starting with one of those bracing exercises, here is a ten-minute practice schedule which is not beyond the means of anyone. All you do is get up ten minutes earlier. Ten short minutes each day—so very little time to devote to Yoga, but how rich will be the rewards, so rich that I feel convinced that many of you will soon want to get up even earlier to devote yet more time to this healthful study.

Ten-Minute Practice Schedule

1. Limbering up for Sideslip   1 minute
2. Sideslip   3 minutes
3. Raised Head and Legs Posture ⎫
        or   ⎬ four times 2 „
4. Leg Raising Posture   ⎭
5. Woodchopper—six times   1 minute
6. Triangle Bend—four times   1 „
7. Triangle—six times   2 minutes

This ten-minute practice schedule can be varied of course, according to your individual needs and the amount of time at your disposal. There may be one exercise which you find you like better than some of the others in which case do spend more time on that one. The schedule I have set out is a mere indication of what can be done with a few minutes set aside for Yoga practice. Do not omit the correct breathing as you perform these exercises and if you would slim do please avoid constipation, as this is one of the worst enemies of the body and of the figure. Yoga will do wonders for your health and your appearance, and for your figure but do please give it a helping hand by watching your diet. The next chapter is devoted to this subject.

CHAPTER ELEVEN

Diet

THE body needs food for two purposes, as fuel to supply our energy, and to repair body tissues. Four elements are needed for the building of the body and for its repair, namely (1) protein or nitrogenous food, (2) carbo-hydrates, (3) fats or hydrocarbons, and (4) minerals, these four elements being found in greater proportions in vegetables than in flesh foods. The most valuable vegetable sources of protein are cheese, soya beans, nuts, peas and milk, and the most wholesome sources of starches and sugars are honey, wholewheat, oats, unpolished rice, and potatoes. Fruits and vegetables, as well as supplying organic minerals and hydrocarbons, also aid in keeping an alkaline reserve in the blood, essential for carrying waste carbon dioxide to the lungs for elimination.

I am not going to try to convert any of my meat-eating readers to vegetarianism (as the practice of Yoga will do this for me in time), but I would say this. That although the meat eater may look strong and healthy he has not the endurance, the staying power, and the resistance to disease of the vegetarian. That a natural diet of fruits, greens, milk and dairy products, citrus fruits, and whole grains is man's ideal and vitamin-packed health-giving diet.

It is interesting to note that all food is originally produced in a vegetable form and is in effect stored up sunshine. Think of an orange. The next time you pick one up to peel and eat it and throw the vitamin-rich skin into the dustbin, think of it as it really is, a parcel of distilled sunshine. And why throw the peel away? Eat a bit of it with the rest of the orange and what you do not eat try grating it into various other foods to add a rich and tangy flavour. It is full of vitamins and added to a jar of honey it adds that extra something.

So to eat vegetables is to eat distilled sunshine. To eat flesh is

116

to take vegetable food secondhand from another animal, and here it is interesting to note that man eats mainly the flesh of vegetarian animals such as cows, pigs, sheep, and poultry, deer, and rabbits. He does not eat the flesh of carnivorous animals.

Why kill helpless and friendly animals? Why subject them to the pain and terror of the slaughterhouse when there is so much goodness to eat from the clean earth? Why take a life away when we can eat fruit off the trees, and all the bounty of the harvest? Why all this violence in the name of good eating? Why not have mercy? The pure in mind do not kill, and the pure in body do not need to kill. Think, do think about it first the next time you cut a piece of steak and carry it on your fork to your mouth; think of the animal who died in pain to provide you with this supper of yours. Are you sure it is worth it? And are fruit and vegetables and nuts not more pleasant to handle than wet and bleeding pieces of a dead animal?

It is interesting to note that once a person becomes a vegetarian and knows the health and purity which results from eating good and pure food, he seldom if ever reverts back to the lower type of food. As he grows spiritually, man ceases to desire flesh foods. Thus man's choice of foods is directly influenced by his degree of mental purity.

And so the Yoga diet is simply to keep as closely as possible to natural foods. This means plenty of nuts, whole cereals, and fresh fruits and juices. From these man can get all the vitamins, proteins, carbohydrates and minerals he needs. From these also he has the means whereby to nourish the cells of the body without overburdening the system with unnatural and alien foods and drinks. It should be noted that even the most perfect system cannot work to the maximum of its efficiency when it is fed with unnatural foods.

What, then, are these unnatural foods to be avoided? These are the refined, processed, tinned and packaged foods, the worst offenders being white sugar, white flour, white rice and any other food from which the vitality has been refined out. Pickles, preserves, sweets and over-salted foods should be avoided, as should anything containing artificial ingredients. This, I know, is not easy if one tends to eat out a great deal. Well-meaning relations and friends hand us heavily iced sweet cakes and sandwiches made with that unwholesome substance, white bread. What can one do to avoid complete social ostracism? That is a problem which you can work out for yourselves, according to your individual circumstances but to all of you I would say this, avoid these foods wherever possible but do not, in the process, offend anyone. Rather eat a piece of cake than hurt someone's feelings. You can leave most of it in crumbs on your plate without arousing suspicion.

The three main rules of the Yoga diet are (1) non-violence, (2) moderation, and (3) attitude of mind. Non-violence I have already discussed. What then of moderation? You must train yourself to eat only what you need and no more. As you proceed with your studies of Yoga you will find yourself taking less interest in food and more interest in spiritual matters. Food no longer becomes a break from the round of work. It becomes a time of refuelling the body so that it may continue to flourish. Remember to chew each mouthful slowly which simple practice will gradually accustom you to taking only as much food as you need, not as much as you think you want. By all means enjoy your food but take it in moderation.

And what of attitude of mind? It is not necessary for you to become cranks and food faddists who measure every mouthful you eat. It is not necessary for you to set up a hue and cry about the needless slaughter of animals for food. Quietly pursue your own course, eat only what is pure and natural and your influence will be far greater on those around you than by any more noisy methods.

I am by no means deaf to the many arguments against vegetarianism that are hurled at me from time to time. They go as follows. If everyone became a vegetarian we should be completely overrun by animals. That without eating flesh our diet becomes dull and uninteresting. That the vegetarian diet is not filling and the amount of food one has to consume to satisfy one's hunger tends to make one gain weight. That one becomes socially 'difficult' and eating out becomes something of a problem. That the fancy health food shops are much more expensive than the other food shops. These are the main objections although there are many more. Let us demolish each one in turn.

Firstly the danger of us being overrun by animals if everyone became a vegetarian. Not true, for the simple reason that animals raised for commercial slaughter are artificially bred to multiply at a greater rate than is natural. If it became unprofitable to breed animals the number of them would be drastically decreased by introducing alternate breeding methods.

From the economic standpoint, if everyone became a vegetarian the area of land used to graze animals for food could be used to raise anything from four to forty times as much vegetable food. Meat is actually no more than very expensive, second-hand, vegetable food. It is a known fact that vegetable foods can be produced much more economically than flesh foods.

Let us then consider the second argument against vegetarianism, that the vegetarian diet is dull and uninteresting. To a cook who is imaginative and adventurous, this need not be so. To one who is not, a flesh diet is equally as unpalatable for a good cook can show her talent with any kind of food. And what can be more colourful and exotic than a plate full of mixed and brightly coloured vegetables topped with grated cheese. What a conglomeration of colours, textures, and flavours. What a wealth of vitamins, and what easily digestible nourishment. Food without killing, surely that is the ideal diet for a thinking man?

The third argument, that the vegetarian becomes socially a difficult customer, is one which the strong minded will choose to ignore. If your ideals and beliefs are against the killing of innocent animals and the eating of their flesh, then you will not mind being misunderstood by well-meaning friends and relatives. Those closest to you will be only too ready to respect your wishes. As far as eating at restaurants is concerned there are many fine and economical vegetarian restaurants up and down the country and if your own particular district has none you could always take your own packed lunch to work. You can always get round the difficulties if you really *want* to.

And the fourth argument that the vegetarian diet is not filling enough and that the extra intake of food tends to make one gain weight? What of this? This is where the eating habits of the Yogis will help you. They chew their food slowly and at the same time very gradually decrease their intake of food until they are eating only enough to keep alive and superbly healthy. More food than this amount is superfluous and tends to put on weight but you will notice that no devotee of Yoga has even an ounce of superfluous fat on him or her.

And what of the last argument, I mentioned, that health food shops are expensive markets and eat up the household budget? True in a sense maybe, if you do not bother to learn vegetarian cookery. If you are a housewife, and your cooking is good and tasty, then perhaps your husband and your children will become vegetarians too. If you live alone you have no one to consider but yourself, and if you are a bachelor, your mother, your sister or even an understanding landlady will come to the rescue. What I am impressing on would-be vegetarians is that it can be done if you really want to. And I am not asking you at this stage to become a vegetarian but merely making various practical suggestions as to how it can be done in the event of your gradually turning against the eating of flesh foods for the reasons I have already outlined.

This is a book about Hatha Yoga and I am writing it mainly from the point of view of your health. However, the body and the mind being inseparable, in showing you how to discipline the one I cannot but mention from time to time the effect upon the other. As Yoga gives your body a new lightness and suppleness you will find that you have gradually become a more spiritual person and food will be of less importance to you than before. You will become more sensitive to the feelings of others and therefore stop to consider the feelings of helpless animals in slaughterhouses up and down the country.

You who long to be slim, to regain your youthful suppleness and vitality, are going to be helped to this end not, as I warned you at the beginning, by any magical or 'crash' diet, but simply by adjusting your eating habits and way of thinking. Where to begin?

First of all remember that our bodies are only nourished by food which they can break down and assimilate and that, ideally, all food should be laxative. This is far from the case, however, and far too much devitalized and unnatural food is being consumed in this modern world with the result that an appallingly high percentage of the population suffers from constipation and other disorders of the digestive tract. As I said at the beginning of chapter eight, the Yogis name constipation as 'the Mother of all diseases', and here we might aptly name devitalized food as 'the mother of all constipation and digestive disorders'.

What is devitalized food and why are the Yogis so against it? Dead and devitalized foods include everything that has been preserved, bottled, bleached, refined, canned, pickled, or polished. When I say avoid eating white flour products, white sugar products, and polished rice you will ask why. What is wrong with these substances? Simply that in their refined state they are unsuitable as foods and are actually harmful to the human body. What is wrong with eating raw sugar, whole wheat flour products, and unpolished rice? They may prove somewhat dearer but who in his right mind would try to economize on good food? And in the case of raw sugar be careful that you are not buying refined sugar that has simply been coloured brown. And try, for a change, to sweeten your food with honey. More easily assimilated than any other food, it is especially beneficial to older people and those of you who are suffering from digestive troubles of any kind.

Being a lifelong honey eater I cannot impress on you too strongly how wholesome and nutritious a food this is. The purest and most natural of foods, it is cheap and plentiful and yet so few people recognize its enormous value.

I seem to hear protests in my ears already. Do you say that you once bought a jar of honey, and you tried to eat it and what happened. It simply would not go down. You dislike the stuff and that is that. But wait. Perhaps you once bought a pound of sour apples. Did you then decide never to buy apples again because you disliked the taste of sour ones? There are very many different honeys. Maybe the jar you once bought was a blended honey, better used in cooking. Why not try one of the dark honeys, brown as a nut, with the strong and heady sweetness of sunshine? Why not try one of the mild, creamy white honeys, thick and subtle flavoured? There is such a bewildering variety of honeys from all over the world that I could not possibly name them all, but perhaps the most delectable of all, though it is a matter of personal preference, are the clover honeys, smooth and mellow as butterscotch, and with an unforgettable bouquet, and the dark-toned, exotic honeys of the Caribbean.

And do not, please, think that honey is always clear golden or biscuit coloured. Honeys are as multi-coloured as a rainbow. The French honey that is gathered from the blooms of gooseberry and sycamore trees is an exquisite sea green. The flavour, need I say, is beyond words. From Brazil comes a black honey, from Africa a clear, pale green, and from Texas comes one of the most unique honeys in the world, the remarkable guajillo honey which is crystal white with a pearly reflection like new milk. Not always available in American "health-food" stores, but to be looked for at any rate, is the exotic lotus honey of India. It is as exciting, as mysterious, and as health giving as Yoga itself. I could go on for a whole book writing ecstatically of the wonder and the glories of honey but let it suffice to say that if you think you dislike honey then try all the different ones you can find. If you fail to find one you like you are indeed unique.

If you feel I was becoming lyrical over honey I am going to be just the opposite about its greatest rival—sugar. Why, I wonder, did we abandon honey, nature's most nutritious sweet food, in favour of dry, sterile, refined sugars? I am afraid that there can be only one answer—sheer ignorance of the basic needs and capabilities of the human organism. Because, up to about the year 1700 sugar was the exclusive amenity of the aristocracy, it came to be greatly prized by the masses as a delicacy. It had a certain social significance as, say, caviare has today. So when a new process was discovered of refining sugar cheaply and in large quantities honey began to lose its popularity as a sweetening agent and became increasingly less available as sugar became more so.

Then physicians in America and Europe began to realize that a tragic dietary mistake was being made and that the over indulgence in artificial sugars was causing increasing ill health. New digestive and nervous disorders began to make their appearance, and the instance of diabetes shot up alarmingly.

Many people do not know that granulated sugars, syrups, treacles, and molasses are artificial sweets. Still fewer people know that they are also powerful stimulants, drugs which are actually habit forming. So used are people to taking them as an everyday commodity that they have come to regard them as harmless, pleasant, and nourishing. I assure you that they are neither harmless nor nourishing though no doubt many would protest that they are pleasant.

The sweets that I have mentioned are manufactured by a process which destroys all their nutritive elements. In the case of granulated sugar the sugar crystals that are formed after the cane juice is treated with the fumes of burning sulphur or heated with bisulphide of lime, are sterile and devitalized. It is just this fact which makes sugar a commodity that will keep almost indefinitely which is a distinct advantage from a commercial point of view but hardly from a health one.

Sugar granules, in their final, highly concentrated form, are powerful stimulants. When they reach the human stomach they oxydize violently upon their contact with oxygen, which produces an explosive effect upon the digestive system and causes an increased activity in the internal organs. White sugar can be compared with a highly combustible fuel that violently ignites, burns with a fierce intensity, and as quickly dies down.

Can you imagine the shock treatment all this activity has on the digestive and nervous systems? And because of this fast dying down the body is aware of a hunger for more and more sugar. It is this fact that makes people often eat as much as a pound of sweets or chocolates at one sitting. The desire for 'just one more' becomes a compulsion, and the more poorly nourished a person is the more susceptible he will be to sugar addiction. For that is what it is, an addiction, no less. That sugar, in the last analysis, can cause serious malnutrition is proved by the fact that although like alcohol, it is a quick source of energy the effects do not last and as the body becomes more and more dependent on these 'quick lifts' it becomes less inclined to eat nourishing food.

To sum up the case for honey and the case against sugar I would say this. That artificial sugars must be broken down by the digestive tract into simple sugars before they can be utilized by the body, and thus they put an undue strain upon the system. The use of honey presents no such problems as it consists entirely of natural sugars that do not have to be oxydized by the digestive tract. Honey is absorbed at once without excessive stimulation or shock to the system and it does not result in a craving for more. Sugar is no substitute for honey as, chemically, it is of an entirely different nature. So why be dictated to by the heavy hand of commerce?

In order to guide you in your choice of foods for your Yoga diet I will here outline the principle vitamins and their easily available food sources. Vitamins, in controlling the body's use of minerals, promotes a balance in the body necessary for the proper functioning of the endocrine glands and the formation of hormones.

Vitamin A

The body uses this vitamin best in conjunction with vitamin D in the proportion of 7–1. The principle sources of vitamin A are cabbage, carrots, celery, endive, lettuce, oranges, parsley, prunes and dried apricots, spinach, tomatoes, and watercress.

Lack of vitamin A produces scaly skin, stones in the kidney and gall bladder, catarrh and sinus infections, poor digestion, and low resistance to disease. This vitamin is essential for proper growth of body tissues, and increases resistance to infections of the urinary and respiratory tracts.

Vitamin B₁

The principle sources are cabbage, carrots, celery, coconuts, citrus fruits, parsley, radishes, turnip tops, and watercress.

Lack of vitamin B_1 results in low heartbeats, poor appetite, gastric, intestinal and nervous disorders, chronic constipation and the enlargement of the adrenal glands and the pancreas. Violent exercise, increasing age and weight, and feverishness all increase the body's need for this vitamin.

Vitamin B₂

The main sources are apples, apricots, cabbage, carrots, coconuts, citrus fruits, prunes, spinach, turnip tops, and watercress. The supply of this vitamin decreases when there is an increase in the consumption of fats and minerals, and is conserved by the intake of fibrous foods.

Lack of vitamin B_2 results in lack of energy and stamina, loss of hair, cataract, tongue ulceration, and disorders of the digestive tract.

Vitamin C

I would mention that copper cooking vessels cause a serious loss of this vitamin. The main sources of it are citrus fruits, cucumber, parsley, pineapples, radishes, rhubarb, tomatoes, turnips, watercress, carrots, and green leaf vegetables.

Lack of this vitamin causes many illnesses, among them being weakness and shortness of breath, palpitations, headaches, tooth decay, peptic and duodenal ulcers, heart disease, circulatory disease, and the impaired function of the adrenal glands.

Vitamin D

This vitamin is stored in the skin as ergosterol, which is converted into vitamin D_2 by sunshine or ultra-violet light. Vitamin D controls the calcium content in the blood; excess of vitamin D results in a number of disorders, including diarrhœa, depression, and severe toxic disturbances.

Lack of this vitamin results in fragile bones, rickets and bow legs, poor retention, and cramps resulting from abnormally low calcium metabolism. Though this vitamin is not found in fruits, vegetables and cereals, butter is an excellent source as is cod liver oil, for non-vegetarians. For the vegetarians there are a number of artificial sources of vitamin D, among them irradiated ergosterol.

Vitamin E

This vitamin is stored in the muscles and fat and as it is rapidly depleted it must be renewed regularly. The main sources of it are wheat germ, celery, lettuce, leafy green vegetables, and parsley. According to recent medical research, lack of vitamin E can produce sterility in both sexes, miscarriage, and loss of hair.

Minerals

The following minerals have been declared essential to the human body by research authorities—calcium, chlorine, copper, iodine, iron, magnesium, manganese, phosphorus, potassium, sodium, and sulphur. I will describe each one briefly, listing the main food sources.

Calcium (alkaline). Daily requirements, adults 10 grains, children 15 grains. This mineral builds strong bones and teeth, aids heart action and the clotting of the blood, and helps to establish the correct balance of vitamin D in the body.

Main sources of calcium are cheese, milk, citrus fruits, green leafy vegetables, carrots, celery, figs, rhubarb, and parsley. Blackberries and cranberries are also a good source of this mineral.

Chlorine. This is a general cleanser of the body and helps to expel waste matter and purify the blood. It also aids in the formation of gastric and other digestive juices. The main sources of this mineral are fruits and vegetables.

Copper (acid forming). The main sources of this mineral, which is necessary for the absorption of iron in the body, are leafy vegetables, fresh and dried fruits.

Iodine (acid forming). As this mineral is essential to the proper functioning of the thyroid gland, deficiency in it results in goitre.

and general glandular disturbances. The main sources of it are green leafy vegetables, carrots, cucumber, prunes, radishes, pineapples, and tomatoes.

Iron (alkaline). This is the mineral that figures prominently in the building of red corpuscles, and which also absorbs and carries oxygen in the bloodstream to all parts of the body. There must be adequate supplies of chlorophyll and copper in the diet to effect the proper assimilation of iron, and some experts consider that a woman needs three to four times as much as a man. The main sources of iron are whole wheat, oatmeal, dried beans, dried peas and dried fruits, green leafy vegetables, cheese, tomatoes, bananas, and fresh string beans. Lack of iron results in anaemia and general fatigue.

Magnesium (alkaline). This is the mineral that keeps teeth and bones strong and hard. It also helps to build cells, particularly of the lungs and nerves, and also helps to form albumin in the blood. Lack of this mineral results in poor circulation, constipation, and acidity. The main sources of this mineral are nuts, whole wheat, unpolished rice, oatmeal, dried fruits, and leafy vegetables.

Phosphorus (acid forming). This is another mineral essential to the building of sound bones and teeth and it also maintains the alkalinity of the bloodstream by the phosphates it forms. The most important sources of this mineral are nuts, particularly almonds, cereals, grapes, citrus fruits, blackberries and cranberries, cucumbers, whole wheat, wheat germ, soya beans, tomatoes, and watermelons.

Potassium (alkaline). This is the mineral basis of all muscular tissue, and is vital to the correct functioning of the liver. The main sources of this mineral are leafy green vegetables, fruits and nuts.

Sodium (alkaline). Though this mineral is important to the body in forming the digestive juices, the saliva, bile, and pancreatic juices, and for the elimination of carbon dioxide, table salt is not the most beneficial source. It is far better to obtain it from its natural sources such as whole wheat, rye bread, buttermilk, celery, bananas, leafy vegetables, and beetroot.

Sulphur (acid forming). This mineral has an antiseptic effect on the alimentary canal, is a constituent of the haemoglobin and keeps the blood purified, and prevents toxic impurities from accumulating in the body. All fruits and vegetables are good sources of sulphur but these should be well balanced with foods of a high phosphorus content such as milk, cheese and eggs, cereals and nuts. Foods high in phosphorus but low in sulphur can lead to improper balance of these minerals in the body.

The above will serve as a useful guide to your future eating habits and with a little experimenting you will find a diet that keeps you healthy and provides all the essential elements you need. Though diet is very much a matter of individual taste and circumstances, here is a list of 'musts' that I learned from my own Yoga teacher.

1. If you do not want anything, then do not eat it even if you think it is good for you. By all means eat meat if you like it but do not eat it merely because you think you cannot live without it. Apart from cheese, eggs, and nuts, the soya bean products, weight for weight, contain more protein than the best steak. Soya bean is not only cheaper and more nutritious but it is also non-acid forming.

2. Eat a little less of everything but do effect this very gradually. Do not starve yourself or suffer hunger pains between meals but do try to cut down on your intake of food.

3. Avoid the 'dead' and devitalized foods, i.e. everything refined, bleached, or preserved. Eat wholewheat bread, raw sugar, or honey.

4. When eating fruit do not throw away the peel. Eat it with the fruit, or in the case of oranges, lemons, or tangerines the peel can be grated to add a delicious and tangy flavour to other foods. Always cook potatoes in their jackets, either baked or boiled. Much of the protein in potatoes is usually thrown away with the peel. And remember the tops of celery, carrots, turnips and beetroots are too nutritious to be thrown away. Cut them up and steam them with the rest of your vegetables.

5. Instead of serving just one vegetable at a meal, cut up several kinds and steam them very slowly in very little water. Do not overcook, in fact many vegetarians prefer chopped or diced vegetables to be slightly underdone. This preserves the natural texture and flavour. Always cook vegetables slowly in a pan with a tight fitting lid and avoid copper cooking pans if possible.

6. Do not drink too much tea or coffee as tannic acid and caffeine are not beneficial to the body. By all means enjoy a cup of tea or coffee but make a mental note that you will gradually cut down your intake. At the same time try to drink more milk, either hot or cold, but please *never* iced.

7. Do not throw away water in which vegetables have been cooked. Why dump vitamins down the sink when they make an excellent basis for soups? With a little seasoning added they are very palatable to drink just as they are.

8. Avoid fried foods especially if you are over forty. When you do eat fatty foods choose what are known as unsaturated fats—corn oil, sunflower seed oil, and soya bean oil. Avoid animal fats such as butter, lard, and dripping, and also avoid olive oil and margarine.

9. Experiment with cheeses. They are all a wonderful source of protein and America alone has many fine cheeses with which to vary your diet to say nothing of the delicious cheeses from other countries. Be adventurous, try new things, and above all eat only what is pure and natural. Do not over-indulge and whenever you are tempted to reach for that chocolate box go to the fruit bowl or the honey pot instead. Try dates instead of sweets.

To conclude I will list the five basic Yoga rules for the maintenance of health and the prevention of disease.

1. Natural wholesome food, enough and no more for the body's needs.
2. Proper breathing and breath control exercises, for the increased oxygenation of the blood.

3. The practice of relaxation of the body and of the mind.
4. Regular exercise to stimulate the circulation and to keep the spine supple and healthy.
5. The practice of concentration and meditation, and the correct method of directing the thoughts towards positive spiritual growth.

CHAPTER TWELVE

Female disorders

IF half the female Yoga enthusiasts I know began their study of Hatha Yoga for the sake of improving their figures, it can be safely said that the other half did so because of menstrual pains and other female disorders. Many females find that drugs do little to alleviate the dragging down pains they have to endure every month, and so year after year they suffer in silence.

But this kind of pain is unnecessary. Yoga can and does help. Practise, at least twice a day throughout the month, the Sarvangasana or Shoulderstand described in chapter four, or if you are unable to do this, try lying down with your feet very much higher than your head. The chief function of this inverted posture in the battle against period pains lies in the reversal of the influence of gravity upon the internal organs. The fluids of the body tend naturally to flow downwards and even the skeleton is subject to downward displacement by the pull of gravity. The downward drag, though it may be held in check by a healthy and active body, is nevertheless always present in some degree.

There is a greater tendency in women than in men to suffer from varicose veins and prolapse of the viscera, this being due to the wider pelvis and larger number of abdominal organs. By inverting the body and holding it in poised stillness, all downward pressure is relieved. Practise the Shoulderstand over a period of time and you will soon begin to notice a lessening of the intensity of your discomfort each month, until after a time it will cease altogether to be a problem. Though a certain degree of slowing down of activity on the first two days of a period is advisable, there need not be any undue resting. Incidentally the Shoulderstand is especially recommended for women after childbirth after a suitable period of recuperation has elapsed, but in all cases do not prolong the posture beyond the point of absolute comfort. No Yoga exercises should be performed during pregnancy or menstruation except the breathing ones, which can be done with impunity.

An especially valuable exercise for women suffering from ovarian and uterine disorders is the BHUJANGASANA, called in English the COBRA POSE. As it belongs to the basic group of essential Yoga asanas it should never be omitted from any practice schedule, no matter what the ailment from which you are suffering. It is not at all difficult and can be performed by beginners in all age groups.

Cobra Pose

1. Lie face downwards on your mat with your chin on the ground, and your legs straight and feet together. Place your palms on the floor at shoulder level keeping your elbows high off the ground.

2. Inhale slowly and deeply and at the same time slowly raise your head, shoulders, chest and upper abdomen, leaving the lower part of your abdomen on the floor. Keep arching your spine as you complete your inhalation, and remain thus for as long as you comfortably can without exhaling. You will feel a strong pressure in the lower part of your back as you push your head back as far as you can. And remember to keep your elbows bent and well off the floor. I have demonstrated the correct position in figure 43, page 133.

3. When the impulse to exhale appears, do so and at the same time gradually lower your body until you are once more touching the floor with your chin.

4. Without pausing, inhale again and repeat the movement and after the second performance of the Cobra relax before you repeat the exercise a third and fourth time.

The Cobra has many benefits and is as suitable for men as for women for it affects the adrenal glands which lie above each kidney, and the backward bend of the Cobra sends them a richer supply of blood and subjects them to a healthy pressure. The Cobra is also beneficial to people suffering from backache, displaced vertebrae, and poor circulation.

FIGURE 43 COBRA POSE

A word of warning though. You may not be used to exercising and your spine may be stiffer than you think so do please be careful while bending backwards in this exercise. Be sure not to jerk your body as you raise it off the ground as you could easily injure a rigid muscle and the pain could last some time. Remember that the Cobra is a beautiful and graceful exercise. As you leave the floor come up slowly and majestically like a rising cobra and under no circumstances must you force yourself to hold the position longer than you find comfortable. Gradually increase the time you hold it until you can remain immobile in the Cobra pose for ten seconds. When you are limbered up you can perform this asana up to six times a day.

While the Cobra is particularly useful to women suffering from dysmenorrhœa, amenorrhœa, leucorrhœa, and various other utero-overine troubles, the overall benefits can be greatly increased by those students able to increase the backward bend. Do not perform the variation until you are able to do the Cobra I have just described with perfect ease and comfort.

Cobra

Variation 2. From the first position, rise into the Cobra with the elbows bent and the spine arched. Slowly straighten the elbows, push the head back as far as you can, so that the bending of the spine involves the sacral to the cervical region. Remain thus for as long as you comfortably can without strain and then relax. When you can perform variation 2 you can, if you wish, omit variation 1 from your practice schedule.

Variation 3. There is yet a third variation of the lovely Cobra Pose for advanced students but it can be achieved by beginners who are athletic or who have been trained in ballet. From variation 2, with elbows straight, bend the spine backwards still farther, gradually bring your toes towards your head to touch the back of your head. This tones the deep and the superficial muscles of the back, and also relieves backache, helping to keep the spine young and supple.

And now to return to another inverted posture to rest the internal organs. For my readers who find the Shoulderstand just a little too strenuous but who need the benefits of this valuable posture, there is a slightly easier posture which has the delightful name of VIPARITA-KARANI MUDRA, meaning literally reverse effect. For short we will call it THE REVERSE POSE.

The radiations which we receive from the earth are negative while those from the cosmos are positive. Thus, when in the ordinary standing position we receive the negative radiation through the soles of our feet and the positive radiation through the top of the skull. In the Yoga poses in which the body is turned upside down, viz. Shoulderstand, Headstand, and Reverse Pose, the effect is just the opposite. Additionally these postures bring an unaccustomed rich supply of blood to the lower intestinal organs.

Viparita-Karani or Reverse Pose
1. Lie flat on your back, hands along your sides and feet together. Inhale deeply and at the same time raise your legs and buttocks off the floor, putting your hands on your hips to steady yourself and keep your body reversed.
2. Place your thumbs just under your hip bone and your hands round the back of your hips. You will find, by practice, your most suitable position of hands and elbows which should be set about a foot apart to maintain correct balance. I have demonstrated Viparita-Karani in figure 44, this position also being the preliminary position of the Plough Posture described in chapter nine.

You will see from the illustration that Viparita-Karani does not require the body to be held straight, but bent at the waistline which should make it easier for some of my readers than the Shoulderstand. Do please keep your knees straight, though, and while in this position hold your body in poised stillness with your eyes closed. Hold it for one minute at first but gradually extend the time until you can hold it steadily and comfortably for ten minutes or more, according to the time at your disposal.

This posture is especially recommended for women who suffer from many kinds of female disorders, and any kind of physical or mental distress during the menopause. Because this posture affects the gonads it controls the ageing processes in the body and helps to restore youth and vitality and a sparkle to the eyes.

Viparita-Karani is very much a beauty treatment for it supplies the skin with an extra amount of blood and so prevents and smooths away untimely wrinkles. This natural beauty treatment is said by some to be worth far more than the costly facial massages in beauty salons which are so beloved of film stars.

Before I go on to your next exercise I would mention here that the CAMEL POSTURE or UTRASANA described in chapter six in connection with backache should also be practised by women suffering from displacement of the uterus and fallopian tubes provided that the displacement is not of a serious order. If you find the Camel too strenuous, try this similar but slightly easier asana which is called CHAKRASANA or the WHEEL POSTURE. Some of the variations of Chakrasana are only within the scope of the most advanced student of Hatha Yoga, but this one is quite easy for beginners.

1. Assume a kneeling position with your knees slightly apart. Inhale deeply and at the same time bend slowly backwards, at the same time raising your buttocks.

2. As you complete your inhalation grasp your ankles and remain thus for as long as you comfortably can without exhaling.

3. When the impulse to exhale appears do so and at the same time slowly return to the starting position. Twice a day is enough at first for this posture but you can gradually increase the number up to six. Lie down and relax after this exercise, and take a few deep recovery breaths.

To end this chapter I will describe a series of slow and graceful movements which incorporate much of what I have described in this chapter. For the busy housewife and mother who has little time to spare, these movements act as a time-saving beauty treatment, a toning up of nerves and muscles, and above all a means of relieving her internal disorders. These movements include the Shoulderstand, the Leg-raising Pose (Udhitta Padasana), Viparita-Karani, and the Plough Posture, and we will call this series of seven movements YOGA IN SLOW MOTION.

FIGURE 44   REVERSE POSE

FIGURE 45   PLOUGH POSTURE

1. Lie flat on your back with your arms extended at shoulder level. Keeping your toes pointed and your knees straight slowly raise your legs until they are at right angles to your body. I have demonstrated the correct position in figure 46, page 139.

2. Still keeping your legs straight and your knees together lower them to the left, thus forming a right angle with the body as I have demonstrated in figure 47. Your feet should be barely touching the floor. Raise them once again to the vertical and then very slowly lower them to the other side, until they are barely touching the floor. Raise them once again to the vertical, remain poised thus for an instant and then very slowly lower them to the starting position without altering the position of your head, shoulders, and arms. Relax before proceeding to the third movement. The first two are simplicity itself and the only point to remember here is that the movements should be done in an unhurried and graceful manner.

It is a good idea to put a slow piece of music on the gramophone, something relaxing and deep-toned, to put you into the right mood for these exercises and to encourage you to move slowly and rhythmically.

3. Keeping your knees together, toes pointed and legs straight, raise them not more than an inch or two off the floor and move them very slowly round at floor level until you are once again in the position I have demonstrated in figure 47. From this position raise them to the vertical, lower them to the other side and, still without touching the floor, bring them round to the starting point. Relax for a few moments and then repeat this movement bringing your legs to the opposite side.

4. From the starting position bring your arms slowly towards your body and at the same time raise your buttocks and legs off the floor and rise into a Shoulderstand, supporting your back with your hands. The Shoulderstand is pictured in figure 6, page 39.

5. From the Shoulderstand slowly bring your legs over your head and lower them until the toes are touching the floor behind your head. You are now in the Plough Posture which is pictured in figure 45, page 137.

46

FIGURES 46, 47   YOGA IN SLOW MOTION

47

6. From the Plough Posture return to the Shoulderstand, and remain poised thus for a few seconds.

7. Bend your body slightly at the hips and at the same time lower your hands, until they are extended at shoulder level. You should now be in the position demonstrated in figure 46 with your legs pointing towards the ceiling. From this position slowly lower the legs and lie flat with the arms still at shoulder level.

This completes the series of exercises. Memorize them before you begin so that your performance is one continuous graceful movement, up and down, side to side, up and down. The benefits of this Yoga in Slow Motion series cannot be too strongly emphasized. From a purely physical point of view all the muscles of the torso and legs are brought into play, particularly the abdominal and dorsal muscles. From a mental point of view it is a good exercise in concentration and control which is vital if the movements are to be performed as they should be, that is slowly, gracefully and above all fluidly. There should be no change of rhythm throughout, and the pauses should match the even rhythms of the movements.

Points to remember. Keep your legs straight throughout, and the toes pointed. Move your arms in rhythm with your legs, and lastly remember your facial expression. It should reflect inner peace and serenity, no matter how hard you are concentrating. And remember to play some slow music while you do these movements. This will not only make it more pleasant for you but will help you to establish an even rhythm. Almost any Beethoven or Mozart slow movement would be suitable but I leave the choice to your personal taste. Yoga in Slow Motion is recommended for toning up the system after childbirth after a suitable rest period has elapsed following confinement.

'Women should practise Yoga that they will have healthy and strong children. If mothers are healthy the children will be likewise. The regeneration of young women means the regeneration of the whole world.

Women who practise a course of asanas systematically, with interest and attention, will have wonderful health and vitality. I hope they will give patient hearing to my earnest and sincere prayer and start practising the asanas from the very day they read the Yoga lessons.

Glory to these women who tread the path of Yoga.'

SIVANANDA, *the great modern saint.*

CHAPTER THIRTEEN

Headaches, eyestrain and stiff neck

PERHAPS it has not occurred to you that nervous tension may be the cause of weak eyesight and eyestrain. When first considered, these two factors may not seem to be related, but it is an established fact that anxiety and nervousness stimulate excessive eye muscle activity which in turn gives rise to symptoms of eyestrain.

If, therefore, you have a nervous temperament, and who has not in these troubled times, and you suffer from symptoms of eyestrain, you may be able to overcome these symptoms simply by learning to relax. Eyestrain is a very common ailment suffered by those who live in a state of nervous tension because slight defects of the eyes, normally tolerated by a calmer person, becomes aggravated in nervous people.

So it is Yoga again to the rescue and your answer to this problem in the first instance lies in reading chapter two again and practising the CORPSE POSTURE faithfully every day for at least ten minutes, and more if you have time. This is not time wasted but time well spent even though it might take you some time to train yourself not to keep glancing up at the clock and listing in your mind all the chores you have to do while you are 'relaxing' on the floor. No, you must be firm with yourself. *Think* yourself into a calm state of mind before you lie down on the floor and practise stretching and relaxing. Then sink slowly into the Corpse Posture, close your eyes and try to empty your mind of all thoughts but one pleasant one. It helps if you are by a fire when you relax and if there is a slow and beautiful piece of music playing in the background, for this will help to put you into a drowsy and peaceful mood. If you find this inconvenient first thing in the morning, try it at night before you go to bed.

Not only will it help you to sleep but it is unlikely that you will wake up with that morning headache which goes hand in glove with tension and eyestrain.

Some of you may find that eyestrain makes your eyes itch or smart, in which case when you lie down to do the Corpse Posture you will find it soothing to lay pads of cotton wool soaked in warm water on your eyelids. You will have to concentrate really hard to coax all your muscles to relax and you will have to be really stern with yourself whenever you find your mind wandering, but mental discipline is not achieved easily but you will find that the rewards for your efforts are well worth it.

In addition to practising relaxation I will describe some very gentle exercises which are designed to develop concentration and mental focusing and also to soothe the eyes and strengthen them. The first of these is a simple exercise called TRATAK or GAZING EXERCISE, and it has two variations. The first one involves sitting down, either on the floor or on a chair but in either case with the spine straight, and gazing at the lighted flame of a candle. The candlestick should be placed on a table so that the flame should be level with your eyes and three to four feet away.

Gaze at the flame while you count to sixty and try very hard not to blink during that time. After the count, close your eyes and try to hold the flame in your mind's eye for a few moments. Open your eyes once more, gaze at the flame, and count to sixty. Close them again and relax.

You may continue the gazing exercise for five minutes but gradually extend the time *ad lib* until you can do it for ten minutes without undue strain. All eye exercises should be done *very gently*, and if any discomfort is felt they should be stopped immediately.

Tratak is an excellent and soothing exercise for the nerves and helps to relax the mind as well as the eyes.

Variation 2. Again sit comfortably with your spine straight and gaze at the tip of your nose while you count to sixty. Under no circumstances should you experience any strain during this exercise and if you do, please cease immediately. If you feel any tiredness, watering or pain close your eyes and relax your facial and eye muscles.

After the count of sixty blink your eyes tightly a few times and keep them closed while you count to sixty again. Open them once more, gaze at the tip of your nose, blink a few times, and then close them again.

This exercise strengthens the eye muscles and increases the powers of concentration by fixing all the attention on one point and through that to the central nervous system, which will be soothed and relaxed. Always try to still the stream of circling thought and these gentle exercises will give you a manifold reward.

1. Here is another exercise which will not only help to relieve eyestrain but the vision will become clearer as the ophthalmic nerves receive a richer supply of blood. Sit down, either on the floor cross-legged or else on a hard chair with the spine held erect but with the body quite relaxed. Without moving the head, lift your eyes and find a small object which you can see clearly and without straining. Then find a similar point with the eyes lowered, which you can see without effort. Use these points to glance at as you raise and lower your eyes alternately several times. Your breathing should be normal. Glance up and down four times, then close your eyes to rest them for a few moments, and repeat the up and down movement of the eyes another four times.

2. Repeat the same exercise but this time move your eyes from left to right without moving your head.

3. The same exercise is repeated with the eyes looking obliquely upwards and downwards with the eyes half closed. Choose a point which you can see high up on the wall from the corner of your eyes, and then find one which you can see clearly when the eyes are obliquely lowered. Repeat the upward and downward movement of the eyes four times, blink and relax for a few moments and then repeat the movements another four times. Rest.

4. These movements are repeated in reverse, starting with a point on the opposite side of the wall from the previous exercise,

thus if you were glancing obliquely upward right and downward left in the previous exercise these movements are reversed in this exercise.

5. And now for something different, though again I must ask that you do this exercise very gently and without experiencing strain of any kind. It entails rolling the eyes very slowly clockwise and then anti-clockwise. Thus, lower your eyes to the floor and then slowly roll them round to the right, continue rolling them upwards until you can see the ceiling and then lower them slowly until you can see the floor again. You must move very slowly making a full vision circle. When you have completed one circle close your eyes after blinking several times and relax. After a few moments repeat the movement in the opposite direction. Repeat this exercise twice each way and then close your eyes and relax before proceeding to the next exercise.

6. This exercise entails changing the vision from close to distant points. It is best done with a candle flame once more which should be placed in front of your face just below the tip of your nose. Holding the lighted candle in your hand very slowly move it away from you, without raising or lowering it, until you can see the flame without straining and without any blur. Raising your eyes slightly look straight into the distance and let your eyes alight on a small point which you can see clearly. This point and the flame of the candle are the two things you must look at in this changing vision exercise.

Look at the flame, which is the closer point, and then look at the distant one. Repeat these eye movements six times then close your eyes and squeeze them tightly. Repeat another six times, blink again and relax.

7. And now for something different again. This exercise will not only help to relieve eyestrain but will also relax you if you are tense and remove stiffness of the neck. It is a specially good exercise when you get up in the morning as many people suffer from 'morning stiff neck' mainly through using too many pillows. It is also a good exercise to practise before performing the Corpse Posture as it has a soothing effect on the nervous system and aids relaxation thereby.

I want you to imagine that your head is too heavy for your body and that no matter how you try to keep it squarely on your shoulders it always rolls away from the upright. Let your head drop forward until your chin is on your chest and then let it roll slowly clockwise several times, up to six. Then repeat the movements six times in the opposite direction. Be careful to watch the muscles of your back and shoulders and your facial muscles as these should be quite relaxed during this head rolling exercise. Keep your eyes open during this exercise and let them follow the direction of your head movements.

Do not be surprised if you hear a grinding and a cracking noise as your head rotates. This is an indication that the linings of the joints in your neck are inadequately lubricated and that there is an accumulation of calcium deposits there. This is a sure indication of your need to practise this exercise which will keep your upper spine flexible and healthy. The Yogis maintain that you are only as old as your spine and that by keeping the spine in a flexible, elastic and healthy condition you can ward off old age for longer than you think. It is worth a little trouble and exercise, is it not, to maintain one's health? So practise this head rotating exercise whenever you have a quiet moment and can perform it inconspicuously.

All the stretching exercises I have described in this book, and particularly in chapter two can be performed in connection with exercising the eyes. The Backbend described in chapter four can be performed so that your eyes follow the movements of your head and are so exercised, and likewise in the Triangle Posture described in chapter ten.

To try something new in this combination of stretching and eye movement, try the *Sideways Bend*. Stand erect with your hands on your head, your fingers laced together. Keep your feet together and your knees straight. Now bend sideways from the waist only for as far as you can, remain thus for a few seconds and then move slowly to the other side. Your eye movements should follow the movements of your head but on no account should you experience any strain. If you do, please stop at once. Eye exercises should always be done very gently and with extreme caution. If there is any pain or watering please blink your eyes tightly and then relax.

And now for one last exercise to relieve eyestrain, which is also a good exercise in concentration and the calming of the mind. It is known as PALMING THE EYES.

1. You have a choice of two positions. For the young and flexible I would suggest you sit down on the floor, cross-legged and your spine held erect. Draw up your knees slightly so that you can place your palms over your eyes without bending your head at all. When you have a satisfactory seated position rub your palms together vigorously to charge them with electricity and place them over your closed eyes. There should be a cupped palm over each eye with the fingers of the right hand crossed over the fingers of the left or vice versa. The fingers should rest on the forehead and the elbows should rest on your raised knees. Do not bend your head.

The second seated position is for those who cannot sit cross-legged on the floor. Choose a hard chair before a table and sit with your elbows on the table in such a way that when you place your palms over your eyes you can do so without bending your head. You may have to use a book or two under your elbows to achieve this position. Having done so rub your palms together vigorously and then place them over your eyes in the position already described.

You can remain in this position for as long as you find convenient. It has the effect of relaxing the nerves and relieving eyestrain, but it can also be used for the purpose of practising concentration. While you are 'palming' your eyes choose a simple object such as a rose you have seen, a candle flame or some similar small thing and hold the image of it in your mind for as long as you can. When your thoughts stray lead them gently back to the object of your concentration.

You can also use this quiet period of 'palming' the eyes to practise the Yoga Complete Breath. As your spine should be held straight throughout this exercise, without bending your head, it is a suitable position in which to practise deep breathing. Breathe in to a count of four, hold the breath to a count of four and exhale to a count of eight. Do this slowly and rhythmically and you will find that at the end of your exercise when you open your eyes you will find a new calmness that perhaps you have never known before.

Palming the Eyes is a simple exercise but perhaps it is the most valuable of all in the relief of eyestrain for, as I said at the beginning of this chapter, one of the primary causes of eyestrain is tension. Remove the one and the other automatically disappears. It would seem unnecessary to say that you should not read or do close sewing if your eyes are tired, nor should you read in bed with the book above the level of your eyes. The eyes should never be subjected to strain of any kind, and all possible care should be taken to protect them from this. They are precious and are deserving of your consideration.

CHAPTER FOURTEEN

Stomach, kidney, and liver complaints

O F all the gems in the rich collection of Yoga asanas there shines forth one which, in sheer beauty, symmetry and grace, outshines all others except, perhaps, the serene Lotus, that impenetrable fortress of repose. I refer to Ardha-Matsendrasana, called in English the SPINAL TWIST, not a very poetic name for what you will see is a Yogic poem of graceful movement. It has the fathomless mystery of Yoga itself, but, also like Yoga it has a bearing and a meaning within our everyday lives. I have said that one is as old as one's spine and I have described all manner of Yogic postures designed to keep the spine healthy and supple, mainly involving forward and backward bending movements. The SPINAL TWIST effects in the dorso-lumbar and lumbar region a lateral twist which not only keeps the spine healthy but which imparts a health-giving massage to the abdominal organs and to the kidneys.

The Spinal Twist is probably one of the most difficult asanas in this book but to write a chapter on stomach complaints without mentioning this posture would be tantamount to sacrilege, so I will describe it in three simple sections, and at the end will describe a simplified version of the posture for my readers who find the Spinal Twist a little beyond them.

Spinal Twist

1. Sit down on the floor, spine straight, legs outstretched and feet together. Raising the right leg place it against the outside of the left knee with the sole firmly on the floor. Stretch out your left arm and place your fingers on the toes of your right foot. Thirdly, place your right arm around the back of your waistline as far as you can, so that your outward facing palm rests on your

149

left hip bone. At this stage please look at figure 48 in which I have demonstrated the correct position. (Page 151.)

This is the first stage of Ardha-Matsendrasana. It is advisable to practise the correct movements of the arms and legs before proceeding to the next stage. Remember that your spine must be held straight and your head up throughout this exercise. Slouching will not only spoil the look of the posture but will drastically decrease its many benefits, so it is as well to perform this exercise before a mirror and check your posture at each stage of the proceedings.

Having arrived at the position as illustrated in figure 48 take a slow and deep breath through the mouth, hold the breath for an instant, and while you exhale turn first your head, then your shoulders, and then your back towards the right. Slowly please, and when your lungs are completely empty you will find you can turn just a fraction more to the right. Remain thus for as long as you comfortably can. When the impulse to inhale returns do so and at the same time very slowly unwind until you are once more in the position in figure 48.

When you have mastered this first stage of the Spinal Twist proceed to the next.

2. Assume the first stage of the posture which by now will be familiar to you, but this time bend your left leg until your heel touches your right buttock. The hands should be in the same position as before. I have demonstrated the correct position in figure 49, page 151.

Again take a slow deep breath through your mouth, pause for a second holding your breath and, while exhaling, slowly turn to the right as far as you possibly can, making a slight extra effort when the lungs are completely empty. Remain thus for as long as you find comfortable, and try to exert as much pressure as possible at the height of the lateral twist. When the impulse to inhale appears do so and at the same time slowly and gracefully unwind. After a slight pause inhale again, and while exhaling turn again to the right, returning to the starting position when the impulse to inhale appears. Lie down after this and relax for a few moments, taking a few deep recovery breaths before sitting up to try stage three of the Spinal Twist.

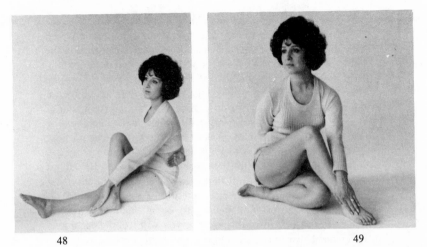

48   49

FIGURES 48, 49, 50 SPINAL TWIST

50   FIGURE 51 SPHINX

151

3. In this third and final stage you assume the second pose as in figure 51 but instead of placing your left arm outside the left knee you place it *inside* as I have demonstrated in figure 50.

Impossible did you say? Not if you practise. Do it slowly like this. Raise your left arm, place the point of your left elbow on your right knee and very slowly glide it along the right side of the right leg until your fingertips either touch the floor or else you can grasp your ankle as in the illustration. The purpose of this last movement is to keep the muscles of the spine rigid on one side while those of the other are subjected to the lateral twist. It is this third and final movement which is the most important one though the mere altering of the position of an arm might seem, at first glance, to be of slight importance. When you can perform this exercise you will feel the enormous difference between stage 2 and stage 3 of this posture.

Having successfully assumed the correct pose at stage 3, again inhale slowly and deeply through the mouth, turn slowly to the right as you exhale, exert as much extra pressure as you can at the end of your exhalation and after holding the pose immobile for as long as you can slowly return to the starting position. Repeat the twist and then lie down on the floor and relax. When you are rested repeat all movements with legs reversed.

Complicated? Yes, I'm afraid it is at first, but once you master the movements you will find it is likely to become one of your favourite asanas. It is beautiful to look at, and when I explain the benefits of this lovely asana you will surely want to keep practising it until you can perform it to perfection. And I assure you that it looks somewhat more complicated on paper than in practice so study the illustrations carefully, one stage at a time, and check your posture before a mirror. I have known many people learn this posture in one or two lessons, but do not be discouraged if you take a little longer. Hurry is a word which is left entirely out of the Yoga vocabulary.

Ardha-Matsendrasana primarily affects the adrenal glands which are situated above each kidney, thus sending them a richer supply of blood. Thus sluggish kidneys are toned and the posture also benefits a congested liver and spleen. Because it calls into play the deep muscles of the dorsal and lumbar region, the spine is strengthened and made more flexible. People with lumbago should also practise it as it brings relief from this and allied complaints, and those with constipation and digestive troubles would also gain much relief from practising and perfecting the Spinal Twist. Nerves and ligaments of the spine are subjected to a healthy pull, and the spinal nerve roots and sympathetic system are toned so that this posture beneficially affects the entire organism.

As though all these benefits were not enough this posture confers on all who practise it the grace and flexibility of a ballet dancer.

In figure 51 you will see a posture which is similar to the Spinal Twist with the exception of the upraised right arm. The right arm is held with the upturned palm at shoulder level instead of being wound round the back of the waistline. This variation of the Spinal Twist is known as the SPHINX, and the exercise may be practised thus as a variation of the more strenuous one just described. And for those of you who find the Spinal Twist just that much too difficult, here is a similar asana which will confer almost all the benefits, but to a slightly lesser degree. This exercise is called VAKRASANA or in English THE HALF TWIST.

1. Sit down on the floor with the legs stretched out and your feet together. Bend the left leg and place the foot on the outside of the right knee, with the sole firmly on the floor.

2. Bend the right leg until the heel of it touches the left buttock. Place your hands on the floor on either side of you with your thumbs and fingertips just touching the floor. I have demonstrated the correct position in figure 52, page 155.

3. Inhale slowly and deeply and while exhaling turn the body slowly to the left. Hold this position immobile for as long as you comfortably can and then, while inhaling again slowly return to the starting position. Repeat the movement to the other side, and then relax. Vakrasana can be performed up to six times a day, and do please remember that emphasis should always be on the pressure at the height of the lateral twist rather than on the number of times of performance.

If, after practising Vakrasana for some time, you find that your spine is sufficiently limbered up for you to be able to perform the full Spinal Twist, do practise it in its three stages until you can do it with ease.

And now for something different. This next exercise, called the KNEELING BRIDGE posture, is a combination of the Frog Pose which I described in chapter seven and the Fish Pose (Matsyasana) which I described in chapter eight. This asana will bring relief from disorders of the stomach, the pelvic organs, and the kidneys, and imparts a healthy pressure to the deep muscles of the spine.

1. Kneel down keeping your knees together and your feet apart. Very slowly sit down on the floor between your heels thus assuming the Frog Pose.

2. Using your elbows, and moving them carefully one at a time, start to bend backwards with your head thrown right back, until the top of your head touches the floor.

3. Lift your elbows from the floor, place your hands, palms together, over your diaphragm, and fully arch your spine. I have demonstrated the correct position in figure 53, page 155.

Remain in this position for as long as you can and all the while arch your spine to the utmost, at the same time pressing downwards with your head. You will find this posture strenuous at first but as you become limbered up it will become easier. Try to increase the time you hold it until you can remain immobile for thirty seconds.

Great care must be exercised when coming out of this posture. No jerks please, and do not hesitate to use your elbows or your hands to support your back as you lift yourself up off the floor. When you are proficient at the Kneeling Bridge posture you will be able to exercise enough control to rise out of it gracefully with no support whatever but until that time please go very carefully.

In addition to the benefits to the lower organs already outlined the Kneeling Bridge posture limbers and stretches the neck, larynx and trachea and thus improves the speaking and the singing voice. It also tones up four important glands, the adrenals, the pituitary, the thyroid and the pineal so altogether

155

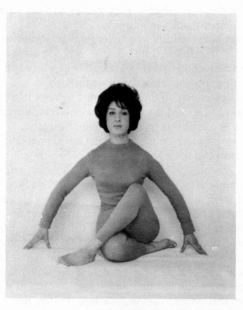

FIGURE 52   VAKRASANA

FIGURE 53   KNEELING BRIDGE

it is one of the most valuable Yoga asanas and should never be omitted from any practice schedule.

I must warn my readers who suffer from heart disease, hernia, and uterine disorders that this exercise is not suitable for them.

A word here about gallstones, an ailment which is becoming increasingly prevalent in this day of synthetic foods and refrigerators. It is well known to those who practise Yoga that there is a thirty-three and a third per cent chance of a complete cure from gallstones by careful dieting, and without surgery.

The worst offenders in this complaint are animal fats, ice-cold drinks, and ice-cream. The substances of which gallstones are made are produced when the body is unable to cope adequately with the amount of fat consumed. To avoid gallstones drink plenty of pure, fresh water, at least nine or ten glasses a day. Take it hot if you wish, with flavouring added, but never, never drink it ice cold. Avoid all foods and drinks straight from the refrigerator, avoid all fried food, animal fats, salad cream, and oils. Plenty of fruit is the order of the day and if you like fresh vegetable juices, so much the better. In this way you will not only avoid gallstones but liver and kidney diseases as well. And remember that animal fats include lard, butter, liver and egg yolk, these so-called saturated fats being high in cholesterol which substance builds up in the arteries and causes untimely ageing.

If you must eat fats then take the so-named unsaturated ones which include the vegetable oils—sunflower seed oil, corn oil, olive oil, soya bean oil, and sesame seed oil, but even then it is not advisable to over indulge in these. If you have trouble with your pancreas, liver, spleen or kidneys be sure to master and keep practising the ABDOMINAL LIFT which I described in chapter five. It is impossible to over-emphasize the far-reaching benefits of this exercise.

Sufferers from all stomach and internal complaints would do well to practise the art of clean eating. Eat only what is pure and wholesome. Study all I have written in the chapter on diet and do not eat anything which has been refined or preserved. Above all, read again chapter five and practise the exercises therein every day from now on. Free yourself from 'the mother of all diseases' and you will be well on the Yoga path to perfect health and everlasting youth, the Yoga path to Self-Realization and Inner Peace.

If the way of Hatha Yoga seems rocky and fraught with difficulties, so that your steps falter and you wonder where all this hard work leads, let the immortal words of the Bhagavad Gita, the ancient Hindu Song of God, inspire you to further efforts.

> '*With the sword of the understanding of thyself thou shalt rend asunder in thy heart every doubt arising from ignorance, and thou shalt achieve thy permanence in Yoga.*'